• SUCCESSFUL
USE OF ENGLISH

FOR FIRST CERTIFICATE

with key

• BY MARY SPRATT •

Oxford University Press

Oxford University Press
Walton Street, Oxford OX2 6DP

Oxford   New York   Toronto   Madrid   Delhi   Bombay
Calcutta   Madras   Karachi   Kuala Lumpur
Singapore   Hong Kong   Tokyo   Nairobi   Dar es Salaam
Cape Town   Melbourne   Auckland

and associated companies in
Berlin   Ibadan

Oxford and Oxford English are trade marks of Oxford University Press

ISBN 0 19 453258 5
ISBN 0 19 453259 3 *(with key edition)*
© Oxford University Press 1990

First published 1990
Fourth impression 1993

Typeset by Wyvern Typesetting Ltd., Bristol
Printed in Hong Kong

Acknowledgements

The author and publishers would like to thank the following for
permission to reproduce copyright material:
David Attenborough and William Collins Sons and Co. Ltd. for permission
to adapt part of 'The Human Invasion' from *The First Eden*; Beryl
Bainbridge and Gerald Duckworth and Co. Ltd. for permission to adapt a
passage from *Forever England*; Nick Baker for permission to adapt a
passage from 'Hold the Front Page' in *The Guardian* 23 December 1987;
The British Council for part of 'Women in Society' from *How to Live in
Britain*; Arthur C Clarke and David Higham Associates for permission to
adapt part of 'If I Forget Thee, O Earth' from *Of Time and Stars*; Roald
Dahl and Murray Pollinger for permission to adapt a passage from *The
BFG* published by Jonathan Cape Ltd. and Penguin Books Ltd.; Nevill
Drury and Frederick Muller Ltd. for part of 'Acupuncture' from *The
Healing Power*; Zohra El Kssmi and ILEA English centre for a passage
from *Families*; Harpers and Queen/National Magazine Company for
part of 'Safari Outing' from *Harpers and Queen* January 1988;
A S Hornby, Christina Ruse and Oxford University Press for an entry
from the *Oxford Student's Dictionary of Current English*; Gillian Rice and
Woman magazine for part of 'Q & A' 16 April 1988; Vernon Scannell for
permission to reproduce 'Uncle Albert'; Time Out Ltd. for permission to
adapt their listings of 25 May 1988.

*The publishers would like to thank the following for their help and
assistance:*
Carol Bryant, Tim Potter, Goodith White.

*The authors and publishers would like to thank the following for
permission to reproduce photographs:*
Barnaby's Picture Library; Catherine Blackie; Britain on View (BTA/ETB);
Children's Express; Creative Company (on behalf of Milton Keynes
Development Corporation); Mary Evans Picture Library; Science Photo
Library.

Illustrations by: Ray Burrows and Axel Scheffler

CONTENTS

HOW TO USE THIS BOOK

STARTER UNIT

The book begins with a Starter Unit which introduces you to the *Use of English* paper of the First Certificate Exam. It also gives you a Sample Paper, so that you can find out for yourself which parts of the paper you need to practise most.

UNITS 1–9

Each unit is based around one of the themes that typically occur in the exam. The themes (e.g. Families, Travel, etc.) are used to introduce and revise vocabulary. Each unit looks in detail at one of the question types that you will find in the exam. The units all have the following sections:

Foundations

These sections introduce the theme of the unit and help you to recall the vocabulary you already know. They also include blank-filling questions in the format of Question 1 of the exam paper.

Exam Training

These sections give you information and practice for each type of question you will meet in the exam. They are divided, where necessary, into sections called 'What you need to know', 'How to prepare', and 'How to practise'.

Grammar Building

These sections revise the main areas of grammar that you need for this paper.

Revision Transformations

These sections are a way of practising the grammar you have just revised in the format of Question 2 of the exam paper.

Vocabulary Building

These sections introduce new vocabulary around the theme of the unit, once again practising the exam formats that you get often in Questions 3 or 4 of the exam paper.

Extensions

There are optional Extension activities after many of the sections. They give you a chance to put the language you have learned into practice outside the context of the exam.

PRACTICE PAPERS 1 and 2

There are two complete *Use of English* Practice Papers at the back of the book. They give you the chance to get to know the paper and to test yourself under exam conditions.

STARTER UNIT

This unit will
- give you more information about the *Use of English* paper (Paper 3) in the First Certificate exam
- help you to focus on any problems you may have in the paper

QUIZ

How much do you know about the *Use of English* paper? Look at the Sample Paper on pages 8–13 to help you find the answers to the questions below. Then check your answers with your teacher or the key.

1. How long does Paper 3 last?

2. Which language skills does it test? Tick (√) the things in the list below which are tested in the *Use of English* paper.

   speaking   ....
   grammar   ....
   vocabulary   ....
   listening   ....
   ability to work to
   time limits   ....
   reading   ....
   writing   ....

   Which parts of the *Use of English* paper do you think you would find easy/difficult? Write your opinion in the gaps below.

   vocabulary questions   (Questions 3 and 4)   ....
   guided writing   (Question 6)   ....
   letter expansion   (Question 5)   ....
   blank-filling   (Question 1)   ....
   sentence transformations   (Question 2)   ....

If possible compare and discuss your answers with a partner.

SAMPLE PAPER

Do the following sample *Use of English* paper within the official time limit.

First Certificate in English

PAPER 3   USE OF ENGLISH 2 hours

1. *Fill each of the numbered blanks in the following passage. Use only* **one** *word in each space.*

It was the middle of the night. Under the blanket, Sophie waited. After a minute or .... (1), she lifted a .... (2) of the blanket and peeped out.
    For the second time that night her blood .... (3) to ice and she wanted to scream, ... (4) no sound came out. There at the window, with the curtains pushed aside, was the enormous long face of the Giant Person, staring .... (5). The flashing black eyes were fixed on Sophie's bed.
    The .... (6) moment, a huge hand with pale fingers came in slowly .... (7) the window. .... (8) was followed by an arm as thick as a tree trunk, and the arm, the hand, and the fingers were .... (9) across the room towards Sophie's bed.
    This time Sophie really .... (10) to scream, but .... (11) for a second because .... (12) quickly the huge hand came down over her blanket and the scream was smothered .... (13) the bedclothes.
    Sophie, hiding underneath the blanket, ... (14) strong fingers grasping hold of her, and .... (15) she was lifted up .... (16) her bed, blanket and all, and pulled out of the window.
    .... (17) you can think of .... (18) more terrifying than that happening to .... (19) in the middle of the night, then let's hear about .... (20).

2. *Finish each of the following sentences in such a way that it means exactly the same as the sentence printed before it.*

    EXAMPLE: It's a long time since he last visited us.
    ANSWER: He hasn't *visited us for a long time.*

    a) It's too cold to go swimming today.

        It isn't ....

b) I'd rather stay at home than go to a bad film.
I prefer ....

c) 'Isn't it a beautiful day?' exclaimed George.
'What ....

d) Although he felt ill, Jeremy still went to work.
In spite ....

e) The meal was so awful that they refused to pay the bill.
It ....

f) Are you still doing your homework?
Haven't you ....

g) 'Anne, what about staying for dinner?' Jane said.
Jane invited ....

h) Somebody will steal your bicycle unless you lock it.
Your bicycle ....

i) I've never been to a safari park before.
This is the first time ....

j) 'I did not take the money,' said Simon.
Simon denied ....

3. *Complete the following sentences by writing in the space provided a suitable word meaning the opposite of the word(s) in capital letters.*

EXAMPLE: There are many countries in the world which used to be RICH, but which are now *poor*.

a) The plane TOOK OFF very smoothly but .... rather bumpily.

b) My opinion is that we need to SHORTEN the working day, not .... it.

c) Tuesday was DULL and wet, but Wednesday was a lovely .... day.

d) People seem to think I'm HARD-WORKING but, in fact, I'm quite ....

e) Many people buy FROZEN food these days rather than .... food.

4. *The word in capitals at the end of the following sentences can be used to form a word that fits suitably in the blank space. Fill each blank in this way.*

EXAMPLES: Pedro lost his job because of his *honesty*.   HONEST
Flavia's *childhood* was the happiest time of her life.   CHILD

a) Hans was embarrassed about his .... because all the rest of his family were tall.   HIGH

b) John had many good points but his .... was his violent temper.   WEAK

c) The student lost marks in the exam because a lot of what he wrote was completely ....   RELEVANT

d) I've never quite understood exactly what kind of .... she has with Andrew.   RELATION

e) He's such a .... person that his students love his lessons.
LIKE

f) They didn't buy the bed because it was so .... COMFORT

g) This newspaper used to be printed ...., but now it only comes out once a week.   DAY

h) That teacher gets very angry about .... work.   CARE

5. *Make all the changes and additions necessary to produce, from the following sets of words and phrases, sentences which together make a complete letter. Note carefully from the example what kind of alterations need to be made. Write each sentence in the space provided.*

EXAMPLE: I be delighted/get/letter/you yesterday.
ANSWER: *I was delighted to get a letter from you yesterday.*

46, Crescent Rd
Wimbledon
London
SW20 5QD

9th May 1989

Dear Jenny,

I write/ask you/you like/come/holiday with us.

a) ....

We have such/nice time together/Scotland last year.

b) ....

So I think/be nice/go somewhere together again this year.

c) ....

We think/visit/islands off/coast of Yugoslavia/August.

d) ....

We go/car from London/Venice/we get/ferry to Porec.

e) ....

Then we camp when we get/the islands.

f) ....

We really look/to go there.

g) ....

We hope/much you be able/join us.

h) ....

Please let/know/we can make arrangements.

i) ....

Hoping to hear from you soon,

Love,

Bill and Betty

6. *Below are some extracts from newspapers, letters, and a poster about the nuclear power plant at Manfredia in Seline. Using the information, complete the paragraphs on page 12.*

DEMOLISH THE NUCLEAR PLANT –IT'S KILLING OUR CHILDREN

ANOTHER **CHILD DIES** FROM **CANCER** – PARENTS ACCUSE **NUCLEAR PLANT**

Dear Sir

I would just like to reply to Mr Hargreaves' letter suggesting that the nuclear power plant at Manfredia should be demolished.

The Manfredia plant provides 500 jobs in this area of the country, where unemployment is very high.

We also have no definite proof that the plant is the cause of the increase of cancer in our area.

We must do some careful research before coming to any hasty conclusions.

Yours faithfully,

Greta Jones

SAVE OUR WORLD CAMPAIGN

JOIN A MASS PROTEST AT MANFREDIA

10 a.m. Saturday 17 July

END NUCLEAR POWER BEFORE IT'S TOO LATE

Manfredia has:
- **increased cancer deaths in Seline by 15% in the last ten years**
- **polluted our seas, beaches and fields**
- **ruined our fishing trade and farming lands**

Dear Sir,

The Manfredia nuclear plant is once more under attack. I very much regret this. I also very much regret the death of the child, Lindsey Green.

I must say, however, as I have said before, that there is no conclusive evidence linking the nuclear plant with deaths from cancer.

Manfredia also provides cheap, essential energy to an area of the country where the only other energy available is expensive imported oil.

We cannot keep our current high standards of living without that cheap source of energy.

Yours faithfully,

James Pollard
Head of the Manfredia Nuclear Plant

Some people believe the Manfredia nuclear plant should be closed because ......

....

....

....

Some people believe the Manfredia nuclear plant should be kept open because

....

....

....

I think the best thing to do ....

....

....

....

....

....

....

....

....

FIND YOUR WEAKNESS

Which questions were easy to answer? Which questions were difficult to answer? Give each question a grade out of 5 (1 = easy; 5 = difficult) and then write down the reason(s) you found it easy or difficult.

QUESTION	GRADE	REASON
1 Blank-filling		
2 Transformations		
3 Word sets		
4 Word building		
5 Letter expansion		
6 Guided writing		

Did your results match your predictions before the Sample Paper on page 7?

NOTE: Try to follow the same procedure in Units 1–9. After you have done a task, think about what you found easy to answer, what you found difficult and why. Discuss it with other students if possible.

You can also use your mistakes to plan your revision by finding your weak areas and then doing as much work on them as you can.

UNIT ONE

FAMILIES

Foundations

1. Look at the people in the pictures below. What do you think of them? Write down the words you would use to describe them.

2. In pairs or small groups, discuss your choice of words.
   Now look at the people again and decide if they would be good mothers or fathers. Which one would be the best parent?

3. With your partner, make a list of the characteristics of ideal mothers and fathers, e.g. *kind*, *loving*, *happy*.

4. Below is a passage with gaps, or blanks, just like the passage you will be given in the first question of the *Use of English* paper. Do not fill in the blanks yet, just read the passage quickly so that you can answer the following questions.

   a The first paragraph is mostly about two people. Who are they?
   b The second paragraph is about one person. Who is this?
   c Does the Elms family live together?

   > Freda and John Elms were neighbours of ours until about ten years ago. They were a happily married .... (1) with three children: Bill, Cathy and Tom. Bill must have .... (2) about twenty-five at the time, Cathy twenty-one and Tom sixteen. Bill left .... (3) when he got married, but only lived a few streets away. .... (4) and his wife saw a lot of his parents, especially after their children .... (5) born, as the parents used .... (6) do a lot of baby-sitting for them. Then .... (7) was Cathy, ... (8) worked in a bank and was a quiet girl. She seemed to have no wish to live .... (9) from home and her parents let her .... (10) whatever she liked. She came in whenever she wanted .... (11), brought her friends home and so on.
   >   Tom was the problem, though. He started doing badly at school .... (12) he was about twelve, then he started going round with a group of boys that his parents didn't .... (13) at all. They didn't say .... (14) to him, though. They thought he ought to learn things for .... (15). But it didn't work out. He .... (16) very thin and very unwilling to do anything. He used to stay in his bedroom .... (17) hours and hours doing nothing or come home at three or four o'clock in the morning. He almost .... (18) talking to his parents. Then .... (19) day they found a note from him on the kitchen table saying he had .... (20) home.

5. Now choose the most suitable title for the passage:

   a A Happy Family
   b Difficult Neighbours
   c The Elms Family
   d Leaving home

   How does choosing a suitable title help you to fill in the blanks?
   Read the next section. It will help you with this kind of exam question.

Exam Training   Blank-filling

What you need to know

The exam instructions: *Fill each of the numbered blanks in the following passage. Use only one word in each space.*

In the first question of the *Use of English* paper you have to fill in the missing words in a reading passage like the one you have just read. This question tests two things:
— if you understand the passage (meaning)
— if you understand the sentence structure (grammar)

The missing words may be things like:
verbs in the correct tense
prepositions
pronouns, nouns
articles like *the* and *a*
connectors like *because*
referring words like *which*, etc.

There is one rule — put only one word in each blank: for example, *can't* is two words.

How to prepare

Remember that you are looking for two things:
— the right word (meaning)
— the part the missing word plays in the sentence, or passage (grammar)

In order to understand the **meaning**, you must read the whole passage before you try to answer any of the questions. The technique of choosing a title helps you to concentrate on the passage as a whole.

In order to use the correct **grammar**, you must look at the position of the word in the sentence, i.e. look at the words before and after the blank.

How to practise

Often you will be able to guess some of the answers immediately. All you need to do now is check them. Ask yourself just three things:
— Is the meaning correct?
— Is the grammar correct?
— Have I used one word?

1. Now look at these three answers for blank number (1) in the passage on page 15. Which one is correct?

    (1) a family
        b couple
        c pair

    (a) and (c) are wrong because they have the wrong meaning: two married people are called a *couple*, so the answer is (b).

2. Now look at these three answers for blank number(2). Which one is correct?

    (2) a was
        b had
        c been

    In English you do not use *have* to talk about age, so (b) has the wrong meaning; (a) and (c) are different tenses of the same verb, so they have the same meaning, but the grammar of (a) is wrong. The answer is (c).

3. Which of the following do you think would be the best answers for blanks (3)–(10) in the passage? Can you say why the other answers are wrong?

(3) a the house b behind c home	(7) a their b there c they're
(4) a Bill's father b him c He	(8) a which b who c that
(5) a been b had c were	(9) a at b apart c away
(6) a to b and c them	(10) a do b making c make

    ## Problems

    Sometimes you can't find the answer at all. You understand the passage, but you can't understand the sentence. This is almost always because you don't understand the grammar of the sentence. There are two methods you can use to find the correct grammar:

Method 1

Look at the words before and after the blank. Often the words around a blank give you clues about the missing word. The helpful words can come before or after the blank. For example with blank number (5) the word *born* gives you the clue that part of the verb is missing and *children* tells you that the part of the verb that is missing will be plural.

4.   Write in the table the word or words which helped you to get the answer to blanks (6)–(10).

	MISSING WORD	HELPFUL WORD(S)
(6)		
(7)		
(8)		
(9)		
(10)		

Method 2

Put any word into the blank, and say the sentence to yourself. Often the sound of the sentence will help you to find the correct grammar. Sometimes trying any verb or noun etc. in the blank helps you to find out what kind of word you are looking for (i.e. if it is a verb or noun etc.). The important thing is to try something. It helps if you substitute a word with no particular meaning and then say the complete sentence to yourself. Try this method using a nonsense word, e.g. *scrudge*. Follow these steps:

– Put the word *scrudge* in the blank and say the whole sentence to yourself. Does it sound the right kind of word?
– Change the end of the word to make it sound like different parts of a verb, e.g. *scrudges, scrudging, scrudged*. Do any of these sound possible?
– Change the end of the word to make it sound like an adjective or an adverb, e.g. *scrudgey, scrudgily*. How do these sound?
– If none of these work, try one of the following:

a preposition	(e.g. *to, with, from*)
a pronoun	(e.g. *he, we, they*)
a possessive	(e.g. *his, our, their* or *ours, theirs*)
an article	(e.g. *a, the*)
a conjunction	(e.g. *when, after, because*)
a relative	(e.g. *who, which, whose*)
an interrogative	(e.g. *who, how, why*)

This method will take a long time the first time you try it, but you will get quicker. And remember, you should only use it when you get stuck.

5. Now look at the passage again and complete the blanks for numbers (11)–(20).

6. Imagine that you are the examiner. You are going to make a blank-filling passage to test some students whose English is not very good. You are going to take some words out of a passage, and then you will ask students to guess the missing words.

    Work in pairs, using the two passages below. Half of the class should use Passage 1, and the other half should use Passage 2. Now, in your pairs, do the following things:
    – Remind yourself of what kind of words the examiner takes out.
    – Look at your passage and choose two words which your students would never be able to guess if you took them out.
    – Choose four words which your students would be able to guess easily.
    – Copy out the passage leaving six blanks where these words should be. Pass your copy to a pair in the opposite group and ask them to find the missing words.
    – When they have finished, look at their answers. Did they find the easy words? If not, why not? Did they find the difficult words? If they did, ask them how they found them.

    Your students should be able to find the easy words. If they can find them, then you have chosen well.

    NOTE: If you are working on your own, choose a passage and put in your blanks. Leave the passage for a few hours (or even overnight) and then try to fill in the blanks yourself. Correct it and if you made mistakes, ask yourself why you think you made them.

Passage 1

My life so far has not been very enjoyable at all. I was born in Morocco, into a very rich family. My father owned many houses which he had inherited, and worked as a fisherman. He more or less took up this job as a hobby because he was very fond of fishing. Before this, he used to be a soldier in the army and he fought in many battles against the Spanish and French troops when they conquered my homeland.

Passage 2

My mother used to work as a nanny for a Spanish family because she disliked the idea of staying at home and looking after her own children. This job was for her an escape from boredom. She benefited from this job by learning Spanish and earning some money for herself, although my father was not at all happy about her working. In the end they had a big argument about it and they decided to get divorced.

Extension   'Teapot'

This is a game to help you guess words. First, the class decides what kind of word they want to guess i.e. a verb, noun, adjective, etc. Then one student thinks of a word, and the rest of the class have to guess the word by asking questions about it. The questions can only be answered by 'yes' or 'no', and every question must include the word 'teapot' in place of the word you are trying to guess.

For example, if you are looking for a verb, you can ask questions like, 'Do you teapot outside?' or 'Do we teapot in the class?' etc.

If you are looking for a noun, then you can ask questions like, 'Is there a teapot in this room?' or 'Can I eat a teapot?' etc.

You will find it useful if a student writes the answers up on the blackboard, so that you can remember what you have asked.

Grammar Building   Modals: possibility, permission, obligation

Possibility: *can, could, may, might, must be*

1. Look at these pictures and make guesses about the people. Give reasons for your answers based on what you can see in the pictures.

    Try to use one of the modal verbs above in your answer, e.g. *She may like dancing*. Below are some questions to get you started.

What might they like doing?
What sort of people could they be?
What kind of lives may they have?
What do you think their jobs or interests are?
What nationality might or must they be?

2. Now read this poem and answer these questions:

    a What did the child think of Uncle Albert?
    b What could have or must have happened to Uncle Albert?
    c Who may Uncle Albert have been?

> **Uncle Albert**
> When I was almost eight years old
> My Uncle Albert came to stay;
> He wore a watch-chain made of gold
> And sometimes he would let me play
> With both the chain and gleaming watch,
> And though at times I might be rough
> He never seemed to bother much.
> He smelled of shaving-soap and snuff.
> To me he was a kind of God,
> Immensely wise and strong and kind,
> And so I thought it rather odd
> When I came home from school to find
> Two strangers, menacing and tall,
> In the parlour, looking grim
> As Albert – suddenly quite small –
> Let them rudely hustle him
> Out to where a black car stood.
> Both Albert and his watch and chain
> Disappeared that day for good.
> My parents said he'd gone to Spain.

Permission: *can, could, may, might*

3. How strict are your parents? Are they more or less strict than other parents?
    Make a list of five things your parents let you do, and five things they do
    not let you do. Begin each sentence *I can* or *can't . . ..*

4. Now imagine that your parents are in a very good mood. You are going to
    ask permission to do some of the things they do not usually let you do. Make
    some very polite requests for permission. Think carefully about which of the
    above modal verbs you should use. Is one verb more suitable than the others,
    or could you use any of them?
    For example: *Could I go to the disco please? I promise to be back early.*

Obligation: *have to, need, must, ought to, should*

5. Which of the following sentences have a real sense of obligation?
    In pairs or small groups, select the sentences which you think involve
    obligation and write a suitable verb in the blank.
    Then decide which modal verbs are suitable to put into the blanks in the
    other sentences. You may use any kind of modal.

    a Children .... go to school.
    b Parents .... go to school.
    c Children .... go to bed early.
    d Parents .... go to bed early.
    e Children .... look after their parents.
    f Parents .... always protect their children.
    g Children .... eat a lot of chocolate.
    h Parents .... give their children chocolate.
    i Babies .... be looked after.
    j Old people .... live at home.

Revision Transformations

Finish each of the following sentences in such a way that it means exactly the same
as the sentence printed before it. The first one has been done for you.

1. It's not necessary for me to go to the wedding because I'm not a relation.
    I need not ...*go to the wedding because I'm not a relation.*...........

2. Jane's father told me that I was not allowed to visit her.
    'You may ....

3. I expect you are pleased about your daughter's new job.
    You must ....

4. Young children are not always easy to look after.
    It can ....

5. It is obligatory for children to start school at the age of five in the UK.
    In the UK children ....

6. Aunt Barbara let Mary go to the disco.
    Aunt Barbara said that ....

7. It was essential for Jeremy to look after his elderly parents.
    Jeremy ....

8. It's very important to tell him the truth.
    You ....

9. It's possible that Sonya and Marco will get divorced.
    Sonya and Marco ....

10. After wars it is necessary for people to have larger families.

After wars people ....

Vocabulary Building   Pairs with opposite meanings

1. Look at the adjectives below. They are all used to describe people. Match up the pairs. One has been done for you.

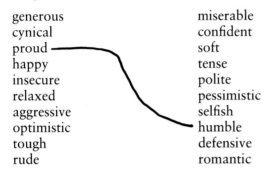

generous   miserable
cynical   confident
proud   soft
happy   tense
insecure   polite
relaxed   pessimistic
aggressive   selfish
optimistic   humble
tough   defensive
rude   romantic

2. Are the above adjectives 'good' or 'bad' in your opinion? Write them out in three columns. The left column should have 'good' words, the right column should have 'bad' words, and the middle column should have words which might be 'good' or 'bad'.

Extension   A Soap Opera

In groups write the background for a soap opera. Decide on the following:
  - when and where the soap opera takes place
  - the main characters and their personality, age, experience, etc
  - their relationship to each other (e.g. friends, brothers, etc.)
  - any dark secrets that the characters may have
  - the title you will give your soap opera

When you have finished compare your decisions with another group's.

UNIT TWO

TRAVEL

Foundations

1. Can you name the forms of transport in the pictures below?

2. How many other forms of transport can you think of? Write down as many as you can. Then, in pairs or small groups, compare your lists. Whose list is longest?

3. What do you think is wrong with transport in your country? In pairs, make notes under the headings:
    - what is wrong
    - suggestions for improvement

    Then compare your opinions with the rest of the class.

4. Read the passage below quickly so that you can answer the following
    questions. Do not try to fill in the blanks yet.

    a What is the main problem that the author mentions in the first paragraph?
    b How does the topic change in the second paragraph?

> Travelling to or from anywhere these days can be an unhealthy and
> frustrating experience. In most cities, air pollution has reached
> .... (1) proportions that we all suffer .... (2) coughs,
> colds and other chest problems constantly. Also our transport system
> .... (3) become dangerously overloaded. Our roads are blocked
> .... (4) traffic jams, while buses, cars, taxis and motorbikes fight
> against .... (5) other to get through. Annoyed and tired, drivers
> drive badly, ... (6) accidents and even murder one another.
> Also, buses and trains are .... (7) crowded that you .... (8)
> hardly breathe or even stand up straight. There are simply too
> .... (9) people wanting to move from one place to another and
> not .... (10) space for them to do so.
>   Town planners, ... (11), tell us that everything will soon be
> different. .... (12) the future, according to them, private cars will
> .... (13) banned .... (14) town centres and be replaced
> by an integrated transport system in .... (15) all vehicles will be
> .... (16) by a central computer and radar will take the place of
> human drivers. 'People movers' – a kind of urban cable-car – will carry us
> high in the air over towns .... (17) car parks, airports, bus
> stations and railway stations. Pollution will .... (18) a thing of
> the past .... (19) all vehicles will have special filters and run on
> lead-free petrol.
>   Doesn't .... (20) sound marvellous? I wonder, though, if any
> of us will be around to see it.

5. Now choose the most suitable title for the passage:

    a Pollution: problems and solutions
    b Traffic: problems and solutions
    c The difficulties of travel

6. Read the passage again and complete the blanks.

7. What traffic problems did the writer mention? Can you think of any more?
    Which do you think is the most serious?
        In pairs, make a list of solutions that you think the authorities should
    consider.

8. Complete these sentences with words from the passage. NOTE: the words will not necessarily be in the same form.

   a A bad accident blocked the motorway and caused an enormous ....

   b Road .... are one of the major causes of death nowadays.

   c I prefer going on holiday in spring when the beaches aren't so ....

   d Cars .... horses as the main means of transport at the beginning of this century.

   e All .... using the roads have to be tested to make sure they are roadworthy.

   f The .... in petrol is a major cause of air pollution.

   g 'You can't leave your car here,' the policeman said. 'You must put it in the ....'

   h One of the main reasons for delays in the city is the amount of .... on the roads.

   i Since cars have been .... from the town centre it has become a much more pleasant place to visit.

Exam Training   Transformation questions

What you need to know

The exam instructions: *Finish each of the following sentences in such a way that it means exactly the same as the sentence printed before it.*

In the second question of the *Use of English* paper, you have to change the grammatical structure of a sentence without changing its meaning. The example the examiners give you is:

EXAMPLE: I haven't enjoyed myself so much for years.
ANSWER: It's years *since I enjoyed myself so much*.

There are three things to notice about this transformation:
     – The order of the sentence has changed
     – The expression *for years* has been changed to *It's years since*
     – The form of the verb has changed: present perfect ◊ past
                                       negative ◊ positive

   You will not need to make all three changes to every sentence in the transformation question, but you will have to make at least one of them. And remember – the meaning must remain exactly the same!

How to prepare

To prepare for this question you must study the different kinds of transformation that appear in the exam. Below are some typical sentences which show the most common kinds of transformation that you will meet in the exam. In each case, think what kind of change the examiner is asking you to make.

1. EXAMPLE: He got wet because he didn't have an umbrella.
    ANSWER: If he **had had an umbrella he wouldn't have got wet.**

    The examiner begins the answer with *If he* . . . This means he is forcing you to make a conditional sentence. You are not asked to find any new vocabulary, only to make changes to the word order and to the verb form.

2. Look at this example. Has the candidate kept the entire meaning of the sentence?

    EXAMPLE: The plate was so hot James couldn't pick it up.
    ANSWER: It was **so hot James couldn't pick it up.**

    How could you improve his answer?

3. In the last example the candidate left something out of his answer; in this example he has put something in that is not necessary.

    EXAMPLE: They are building a new terminal at Heathrow.
    ANSWER: A new terminal **is being built by them at Heathrow.**

    Which words can you take out to improve his answer?

4. In this example the examiner has kept the same word order, but changed the verb form to negative. This should warn you that you will have to change an expression if you want to keep the same meaning. Which word must you change?

    EXAMPLE: She remembered to give you the key, didn't she?
    ANSWER: She didn't .... ?

    How would you complete the sentence?

5. Sometimes the examiner changes the expression for you; you must show that you can use the new expression correctly. Look at these two examples:

    EXAMPLE: Sally does not like people calling her Mrs Jones.
    ANSWER: Sally wishes ....

    EXAMPLE: 'I am sorry I didn't buy the old boat,' said Charles.
    ANSWER: Charles regretted ....

    How should you complete these sentences?

6. You will probably also have to change direct speech into indirect speech, or vice-versa.

    EXAMPLE: 'Where is the front door?' Jane asked.
    ANSWER: Jane asked ....

    How should you complete this sentence?

7.   Here are some sentences for you to practise – without help this time!

a   Travelling by train is usually quicker than travelling by road.
It is not ....

b   Bill didn't go to work because there was a transport strike.
If there ....

c   I prefer flying to going by boat.
I'd rather ....

d   We haven't got enough money to fly to Madrid.
It's too ....

e   It was such a difficult journey that it took John nearly ten hours.
The journey ....

f   It's not always necessary to show your passport at the border.
You ....

g   If a new bridge is not built, the traffic problems will get worse.
Unless ....

h   The new motorway to the coast is still being built.
They are still ....

i   'Why don't you go to the island by hydrofoil?' Tim suggested.
Tim suggested ....

j   'Don't forget to take all your hand luggage with you,' the air hostess told the passengers.
The air hostess ....

Extension

Look at the words below which are taken from this unit. In pairs or groups, use them to make an imaginary story. You must use all the words, in any order, but you can change their grammar, e.g. singular to plural, present to future tense, etc. You can also add any other words you need. When you have finished your story tell it to another pair or group.

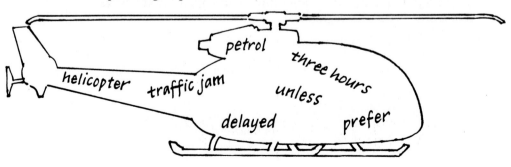

Grammar Building   Some past tenses and the present perfect

1. Look at the sentences below. They tell a story, but they are in the wrong order. Can you put them into the correct order?
    Underline the verb forms and say what kind they are, e.g. simple past, past continuous, present perfect, *used to*, etc.
    Can you change the verb form to another tense without changing the meaning?

    a When I travelled by bicycle, I was fit. Now I have become fat.
    b I was very proud of my motorbike, and I cleaned it every Sunday.
    c Then I got a better job and bought a motorbike.
    d I broke my leg; it has never fully recovered.
    e One rainy day, I was riding it when I had an accident.
    f While I was searching for a car, I came across an old red van.
    g In the old days I used to travel everywhere by bicycle.
    h I have never been able to remember how it happened.
    i So I decided to buy a car instead.
    j I fell in love with the van and bought it. I have had it ever since.

2. Look at the following sentences and write the correct form of the verb in brackets. The first one has been done for you.

    a I still (not/fly) in a helicopter.
       I still have not flown in a helicopter.
    b You (never/be) on a ski-lift, have you?
    c For the last six months I (drive) to work by car.
    d She (go) to Egypt ten years ago.
    e Because of bad weather, the ferry (operate) for only six days last month.
    f Since I (buy) my car, I have been out much more than before.
    g When he was a young man, he (never/travel) by train.
    h I (have) a motorbike since 1986.
    i Our great grandparents (never/dream) that men would go to the Moon.
    j From 1984–87 they (have) a van. Now they have a jeep.
    k They (not/buy) their plane tickets yet.
    l They (already/build) two bridges over the river and now they are building a third.
    m you (ever/visit) Russia?

3. 'Were you an artist?' In this game one student pretends to be a famous person in the past who is now dead. The other students have 20 questions to discover who he or she was. He or she may only answer 'yes' or 'no' to their questions.
    Students take turns to ask questions. Each time that a student receives a 'yes' answer, the student gets a free question and may consult with the rest of the class about what to ask. At all other times, students have to think of questions on their own.

Revision Transformations

Finish each of the following sentences in such a way that it means exactly the same as the sentence printed before it.

1. I last travelled by tram when I was a child.
   I haven't ....

2. Bill Brown started flying planes ten years ago.
   Bill Brown has ....

3. They have already banned lorries from the centre of some cities.
   Lorries ....

4. How long is it since they first used battery-powered cars?
   When ....

5. Public transport used to be cheaper than it is now.
   Public transport isn't ....

6. I've never been on a transatlantic flight before.
   This is ....

7. My grandmother used to cycle more than she does now.
   My grandmother doesn't ....

8. Before the bypass was built, you couldn't cross the High Street safely.
   Now the bypass ....

9. This airline used to be so dangerous that very few people used it.
   This used to be ....

10. The superjet flew from London to New York in only two hours.
    It only took ....

Vocabulary Building   Phrasal verbs

1. The passage below is full of phrasal verbs. Read it carefully and list all the phrasal verbs with *get* that you can find in the passage. Write them in the infinitive form and make sure that you write all the parts down. The first one has been done for you.

   'Get up! It's a lovely day. The sun is shining – we're going to the coast! You can't get out of it!'
       I looked at the clock. It was only half past five in the morning. I usually get on well with my sister, but sometimes . . .!
       'I don't want to sit in a car and drive for hours. I'm ill,' I complained.
       'Rubbish!' she said. 'You've got over your cold. Come on!'
       Oh well! Obviously I could not get on with my studying today. I really

had to get through that exam, but never mind – studying always gets me down.

I went downstairs and put my coat on. Then I remembered! The car was at the garage. We would not get it back until tomorrow. It had a flat tyre. I took my coat off and went upstairs. I got into bed again with a smile on my face. It was going to be a lovely day after all!

—to get up — —   — — — — — — — —   — — — — — — — —

— — — — — — — —   — — — — — — — —   — — — — — — — —

— — — — — — — —   — — — — — — — —   — — — — — — — —

2.   Now match the phrasal verbs with the definitions below. Be careful: one verb has two different meanings!

to rise from bed   -
to pass an exam successfully   -
to make somebody depressed   -
to recover possession of something   -
to have a good relationship with somebody   -
to avoid doing something   -
to recover from something   -
to make progress with something   -
to climb into   -

Extension   'Means of transport'

In this game one group describes a means of transport and the other group has to guess what is being described. Use the pictures above to help you; your means of transport might be a machine or an animal.

Divide the class into two groups. Each group thinks of a different means of transport for each member of the group. Each member then writes a description of their means of transport in no more than five short sentences, without using its name.

The groups take it in turns to read out their descriptions to the other group, stopping after each sentence to give the other group a chance to guess. If the description is very good, the other group might be able to guess after the first sentence! For example:

DESCRIPTION: You sit on it and push two pedals with your feet.
ANSWER: It's a bicycle.

NOTE: In order to encourage good descriptions and quick guesses you can use the following scoring system:

The 'describing' group scores 5 points if the other group guesses correctly after hearing only the first sentence. It scores 4 points after the second sentence, 3 after the third, 2 after the fourth, and 1 after the fifth.

The 'guessing' group also benefits from guessing quickly, since it is given half of the 'describing' group's score, e.g. when the 'describing' group scores 4 points (for guessing after the second sentence) the 'guessing' group also scores 2 points.

UNIT THREE

WORK

Foundations

1. Look at these photos and number them (1)–(6), according to which you think best (1) and least (6) describes the work situation in your country.

2. Compare and discuss your numbering with a partner.

3. Read the passage below quickly so that you can answer the following questions. Do not try to fill in the blanks yet.

a What is the relationship between Christopher, Tom and Tony?
b Do they all have jobs?
c Do they all want to have jobs?
d Is the author sympathetic or unsympathetic towards them?

> As a working man, Christopher MacLean counts himself among the
> fortunate. .... (1) the exception of two years on the dole when he
> was just married, he has been .... (2) in the docks .... (3)
> a boat handler for the best part of twenty years. A man needs to work; it
> is his right. He doesn't have any respect .... (4) himself
> .... (5) he cannot organize his life and support his own family.
> His eldest boy, Tom, ... (6) is married and lives with his wife
> and children .... (7) the road in a decaying pre-war house, is
> employed .... (8) the moment, ... (9) there is no
> guarantee of how .... (10) it will last. Before that he was out of
> .... (11) for two years. He got himself qualified as a welder and
> .... (12) as he was about to change from apprenticeship to full
> wages, they gave him the sack. .... (13) broke his heart.
> Christopher's younger son, Tony, has never .... (14) a job.
> Christopher understands why his son can't get .... (15) of his
> bed until the afternoon, ... (16) it irritates him, hearing young
> Tony wandering around the .... (17) in the small hours, turning
> night into .... (18). Tony has never asked his father or brother
> .... (19) a penny, but he gets depressed because he is an able
> man, a willing .... (20) who wants to work.

4. In this passage there is one concern which affects the lives of all the MacLean family. Which of the following phrases is the best description of that concern?

a Working in the docks
b Supporting the family
c The threat of unemployment

5. Read the passage again and complete the blanks.

6. Complete these sentences with words or phrases from the passage. NOTE: The words will not necessarily be in the same form.

a It will take me six years to .... as a doctor.
b She thought her boss had given her the ....
c Many people work hard to .... their families.
d I'm .... at the moment. I've looked everywhere for a job and just can't find one.
e He got very .... when he was turned down for every job he applied for.
f I've been .... by this firm for the last twenty-five years – ever since I left school.

Extension Jobs quiz

One person in the class thinks of a job (e.g. secretary, baker) and the other students have to guess the job by asking a maximum of twenty questions. For example:

   – Do you need qualifications?
   – Do you do the job outdoors?
   – Do you need to be physically strong?

The person thinking of the job can only answer 'Yes' or 'No'. If the other students guess the job by asking twenty or fewer questions, they are the winners. If not, the person thinking of the job is the winner.

Exam Training Vocabulary questions (1)

What you need to know

In the *Use of English* paper you will find questions which test your knowledge of vocabulary. These questions will test *word families* and *word building* (see Unit 4) or they will test other areas of vocabulary which may include:

opposites	e.g. *happy, sad*
preposition phrases	e.g. *in two, in half, in pieces*
word sets	e.g. *day, year, month, week*
compound words	e.g. *big-headed, kindhearted*
phrasal verbs	e.g. *to get through, to get out of*

There are several different kinds of exercise which test vocabulary, and so the exam instructions are not always the same. Look carefully at the examples in this section, and in the Exam Training section in the next unit.

How to practise

1. Look at the groups of words below and say which of the above areas of vocabulary they belong to, e.g. (a) = preposition phrases.

   (a) on time
       in time
       out of time

   (b) to give away
       to give back
       to give in
       to give out
       to give up

   (c) nurse
       hospital
       patient
       illness
       doctor

   (d) full-time
       employment agency
       part-time
       working-class
       man-made

   (e) rich/poor
       young/old
       clever/stupid
       loud/soft
       easy/difficult

2. Here are two examples of vocabulary questions. Complete them as indicated.

Complete the following sentences with **one** suitable word meaning the opposite of the word in capital letters.

a John much prefers being EMPLOYED to being ....
b Alfredo did a number of TEMPORARY jobs before he managed to find a .... position.
c The first shop Jane opened was a big SUCCESS but the second was a total ....
d The management said salaries had INCREASED but official statistics showed they had ....
e Many people would rather work .... than FULL-TIME.

Complete the following sentences with **one** appropriate word connected with the subject of **money**.

f They refused to accept a cheque so I had to pay in ....
g When Mr Jumilla retired he received a .... of £1000 a year.
h When Lizetta started with the company her .... was only £5000 a year. Now it's twice that.
i If you want a new car why not go and see your bank manager about a ....
j Pierre is very worried because he is in .... and nobody will lend him any money.

---

3. Compare your answers with a partner's. Now look back at the five areas of vocabulary given on page 35. Which area of vocabulary was being tested in each exercise?

How to prepare

It is difficult to prepare specifically for this part of the exam, since there are many possible items of vocabulary which might be tested. Two good pieces of advice, however, are:

  – Read, read, read! The more you read in English, the better prepared you will be for the exam. Read as many different types of text as you can: newspapers, pop magazines, graded readers. You should be able to find all these without too much difficulty.
  – Keep vocabulary lists of unknown words in a special section of your file or exercise book. You could organize these lists as follows:

WORD	MEANING (IN ENGLISH OR YOUR OWN LANGUAGE)	PART OF SPEECH	EXAMPLE SENTENCE
dole	money given to the unemployed ἐπίδομα ἀνεργίας	noun	Some people have been on the dole for years.

To help you to remember the words on your list, you could occasionally read the list over and, for example:

 — find all the words connected with a particular topic
 — find all the opposites
 — find all the compound words
 — find all the adjectives, nouns or verbs
 — find all the words you like or dislike
 — find all the words that remind you of a part of your life – your childhood, hobbies, family, school, etc.
 — test and quiz one another on the meaning of the words
 — work or play with these words in any other way you can think of
 — build families for new words – see Unit 4, page 43

Extension   Match the people to the jobs

Imagine that these fictional characters suddenly needed to get a job. What do you think would be the best job for them? And why? In pairs or small groups, choose a job for each of them from the list below, or from your head. Make sentences like:

I think Dracula would make a good nurse or butcher because he's fond of blood.

PEOPLE: Dracula, Superwoman, Cinderella, Father Christmas, Batman
JOBS: postman, computer programmer, pilot, teacher, butcher, manager, nurse, engineer, vet, travel agent, fashion model, president, astronaut, antique dealer

Grammar Building   Comparisons: *so*, *such* and *too*

1. Look at the sentences below and tick (√) them if you agree with them and
    cross (×) them if you disagree with them.

    a A nurse needs to be fitter than a teacher.   (   )
    b Gardeners live longer than businessmen.   (   )
    c Journalism is the toughest job in the world.   (   )
    d Teachers are usually more patient than shopkeepers.   (   )
    e The least stressful jobs are the most boring ones.   (   )
    f It is less tiring to sit at a desk than to stand on a factory floor. (   )
    g Doctors are cleverer than dentists.   (   )
    h The cleverest workers do not always get promoted.   (   )
    i Being a secretary is more interesting than working at home.   (   )
    j Police officers are always busier than traffic wardens.   (   )

2. Look at the sentences in 1. again and, depending on whether you agreed or
    disagreed with the statement, make sentences using *as . . . as* or *not as/so . . .
    as*. For example:

    A teacher needs to be as fit as a nurse.
    A teacher does not need to be as fit as a nurse.

    or

    Businessmen live as long as gardeners.
    Businessmen do not live so long as gardeners.

3. Look at these sentences and fill the blanks with *so*, *such*, or *too*.

    a It was .... an interesting job that he applied for it.
    b There were .... many applicants that he decided not to apply for
       the job.
    c He worked .... hard that he made himself ill.
    d Her job was .... a well paid one that it was very difficult to give
       it up.
    e He had .... little spare time that he decided to change his job.
    f The job was .... hard for him to finish.
    g Her work was .... boring that she thought she would go mad.
    h His job was .... hard work that he resigned.
    i She worked .... well that she got promoted.
    j She had .... much work to go out that night.

Revision Transformations

Finish each of the following sentences in such a way that it means exactly the same as the sentence printed before it.

1. John's salary was so low that he demanded a pay rise.
   John had ....

2. 'My other job was more interesting than this one,' Christine said.
   Christine said that this job wasn't ....

3. Paul wasn't healthy enough to become a soldier.
   Paul was ....

4. The new director didn't have as much work as he wanted.
   The new director wanted ....

5. Tom had such an exciting time working abroad that he never came back.
   The time Tom spent ....

6. She inherited such a lot of money that she didn't need to work.
   Her inheritance was ....

7. Maureen didn't have enough holiday to visit her aunt in Australia.
   Maureen's holiday ....

8. I've never had such a marvellous opportunity before.
   This is ....

9. Toshi worked harder than Makiko.
   Makiko didn't work ....

10. The training course was not so interesting as he had expected.
    He had expected ....

Vocabulary Building   Word Sets

1. Without looking back through the unit, write down all the words you can think of related to the topic **work**.

2. Now write the words into your vocabulary books, following the advice about organizing word lists on pages 36–37.

3. With a partner choose one of the ideas for remembering lists of words (for example, finding as many opposites as possible) and do it using the list of words you have just made.

Extension   'The best job for me!'

Look at the following list of jobs and note down what you think the advantages and disadvantages of each job would be.

JOB	ADVANTAGES	DISADVANTAGES
ice-cream seller		
lion-tamer		
weather-forecaster		
cowboy/cowgirl		
fire-fighter		
window-cleaner		

Which job would you choose to do? In pairs or small groups, discuss why you would like or not like to do these particular jobs.

Finally, talk about your real job preferences.

UNIT FOUR

THE FUTURE

Foundations

1. Look at the pictures below. What do they make you think of?

2. Would you like to live on the moon? What would you like about being there? What would you miss most about life on Earth? In pairs or small groups, make a list of the things that you would like and the things that you would miss.

3. Read the passage below quickly so that you can answer the following questions. Do not try to fill in the blanks yet.

    a There is a change of topic from paragraph one to paragraph two. What is it?
    b Where is the 'Colony' and where is 'home'?

    > And then Father began to tell Marvin the story. There were .... (1) things he did not understand: it was impossible for .... (2) to imagine life on the planet he had never seen. Nor could he understand why it had .... (3) destroyed in the end, leaving the Colony alone. .... (4) he did understand the pain of .... (5) last days when the Colony had learnt at .... (6) that the supply ships would never again come .... (7) through the stars with presents from home. One by one the radio stations on Earth had .... (8) calling: the lights of the cities had died, and .... (9) were alone at last as no men .... (10) been alone before, carrying the future of the race in .... (11) hands.
    >   So, at last, Marvin realized that he .... (12) never walk beside the rivers of .... (13) lost world or listen to the thunder .... (14) its hills. Yet one day – how far ahead – .... (15) children's children would return. The winds and the rains would carry the poisons .... (16) the burning lands down to the sea, and in the depths of the sea they .... (17) harm no living thing. Then the great spaceships .... (18) were still waiting here on the silent, dusty plains could lift off once .... (19) into space, along the road that led .... (20) home.

4. Now choose the most suitable title for the passage:

    a Marvin learns about life on a strange planet
    b Marvin learns why he will never see the planet Earth
    c Marvin doesn't understand why the supply ships didn't come back
    d Marvin's father explains why the Colony was destroyed

5. Read the passage again and complete the blanks.

6. Use the words below and any others you need to retell the story of what happened to the Earth and its people.

supply ships	poison
cities	radio stations
burn	planet
colony	alone

7. Read through the passage again and note down all the words related to space and the Earth.

8. List any other events that you think could happen in the world in the next hundred years. Compare and discuss your lists.

Extension   'Ten items in a trunk'

In pairs or small groups, decide what ten items you would put in a small one metre square trunk as a record of the 20th Century. This will then be put in a satellite to drift in space.

   Justify to the other groups why you have chosen what you have chosen, why you think those particular things are worth saving, etc.

Exam Training   Vocabulary questions (2)

In Unit 3 you looked at various areas of vocabulary. The questions in the *Use of English* paper also test your knowledge of another area of vocabulary, word families, that is the ways that words are 'built' or how you make adjectives or verbs from nouns etc. For example:

Her teacher .... her to plan for her future.   COURAGE

   In English, there are word beginnings (e.g. *un-*, *dis-*, *over-*) and word endings (e.g. *-ful*, *-ment*, *-ing*) which can be added to a word to make new words. Look at this example:

   un-
   fashion   *unfashionable*
   -able

The spelling of some words will need to change:

   argue
     -ment   *argument*

   lazy
     -ness   *laziness*

NOTE: Not all words are built like this. For example:

   long (adj)   →   length (noun)
   broad (adj)   →   breadth (noun)

   You will need to watch out for these and write them down in your vocabulary books.

1. There are a lot of different word beginnings and word endings. You will find them very useful to know – they are a quick and useful way of increasing your vocabulary!

Imagine, for example, that you have just learnt the word *friend*. How many words can you build, using the beginnings and endings given below?

un-   - ship
                   -ly
     friend -less
over-   -ness

If you record these words in your vocabulary book in the way suggested on page 37, instead of only learning one word, you will have learnt eight!

2. In the following section, look at the groups of word endings and word beginnings. Use one of them with each word to make a new word. Make a note of any spelling changes. Then answer this question about each one:
    – What type of words (e.g. nouns, adjectives, verbs) do these beginnings/endings make?

    NOTE: It may be possible to use two different beginnings/endings with one word.

    a   *dis-, il-, im-, in-, ir-, non-, un-*
able	happy	loyal	smoker	mature
certain	like	possible	convenient	proper
capable	logical	responsible	dependent	kind
honest	agree	relevant	legal	

        What letters do you use *im-, il-,* and *ir-* in front of?

    b   *-ity, -ment*
able	encourage	probable	possible
develop	responsible	employ	capable
mature	govern	agree	

    c   *-ness, -hood, -ship*
dry	hard	friend	friendly	companion
child	childish	sad	happy	neighbour
widow	owner	fresh	stale	short
soft	light	kind		

    d   *-er, -or, -ist*
act	play	work	govern	own
employ	piano	violin	guitar	type
write	physics	biology		

    e   *-en, -ify, -ize*
black	popular	simple	broad	solid
sad	clear	hard	soft	light
short	long	legal	fresh	

f *-ful, -ish, -less, -y*

beauty	dust	forget	ice	friend
child	hope	fool	joy	care
sun	wind	rain		

3. Here are two examples of a vocabulary question. Complete them as indicated.

a The words in capitals at the end of each of the following sentences can be used to form a word that fits suitably in the blank space. Fill each blank in this way.

EXAMPLE: Everybody appreciated his *kindness*. KIND

1 He said he had never seen such a .... place. BEAUTY
2 Because the road was wet, she had to drive very .... CARE
3 .... is often said to be the happiest period of your life. CHILD
4 The .... of an Olympic swimming pool is fixed by the Olympic Committee. LONG
5 The audience was delighted by the performance of the .... MUSIC
6 She had wanted to be an .... ever since she was a girl. ACT
7 The firm demanded his .... after his shocking behaviour. RESIGN
8 I feel much more .... since I've been taking vitamin pills. ENERGY

b Complete the following sentences with one suitable word formed from the word in capitals and **opposite** in meaning.

EXAMPLE: The judge's decision was bad and *unfair*. FAIR.

1 That silly fool is .... of finding his way home! CAPABLE
2 It is a mistake to .... someone because of what they wear. LIKE
3 The girl looked .... at her mother and began to cry. HAPPY
4 'Driving after drinking is a sign of ....,' said the judge. RESPONSIBLE
5 Losing the keys is bad enough, but losing the car is a matter of total .... ! CARE
6 It is .... to give a young person too much money. WISE
7 I don't like what he says. In fact, I .... with it. AGREE
8 There are special parking spaces for .... drivers. ABLE

Extension   Associations

Below are many adjectives used to describe people's different qualities. In pairs or small groups, build as many nouns as you can from them, e.g. *happy* becomes *happiness*.

intelligent	weak	strong	certain
fair	honest	kind	loyal
true	sad	cruel	responsible
equal	happy	stupid	friend
wise	patient	clever	free

   Now choose five of the nouns and say who they make you think of. Then write sentences like this:

   I associate intelligence *with Socrates.*

Compare your answers.

Grammar Building   Future forms; conditionals in the future

Future forms

1.   Look at the sentences below. They all refer to the future, but they use different verb forms. Underline the verb form and say what kind it is, e.g. simple present, present continuous, *will*, or *going to*, etc.
   Can you change the verb form without changing the meaning?

   a A spaceship will arrive on Venus next year.
   b Those rockets are going to crash into one another. Just look how close they are!
   c The next spaceship is arriving on Venus at 5 p.m.
   d This rocket reaches Venus next year, before continuing on its planned trip to Mars.
   e Look, there's a shooting star! I'll get my telescope.
   f She's going to meet me on the moon at 8 o'clock next Thursday.
   g I'm visiting the moon next week.
   h The anniversary of the first manned landing on the moon is next week.

2.   Look at the following situations. Make sentences using an appropriate tense.
   For example, if you are inviting a friend to a party you've organized in your house on the moon next week, you will say:

   I am having a party in my house on the moon next Thursday. Will you come?

   a You are telling a customer the times of next week's Moon rocket transport service.

b You are making a news broadcast describing the American space agency's future space programme.

c You are giving your opinion on man's progress in space exploration.

d You are reporting on the probable weather for a rocket launch in three hours' time.

e You are replying to a friend who has asked for a lift to the moon.

f You are telling a friend about your plan to fly to Pluto next Monday.

Conditionals

3. Divide the class into two groups, A and B, and divide each group into pairs. Each pair will write three simple conditionals about the future, for example:

If I study hard, I will pass First Certificate.
If you marry young, you will have a big family.

Each pair then tells a pair in the other group the second part only of their sentences, for example:

. . . you will have a big family.

The other pair has to guess the first part of the sentences. Write the sentences down in your books or on the blackboard.

4. Now change the sentences you have made using *unless*, for example:

Unless you study hard, you won't pass First Certificate.
Unless you marry young, you won't have a big family.

Revision Transformations

Finish each of the following sentences in such a way that it means exactly the same as the sentence printed before it.

1. Unless Victor comes soon he will miss the plane.
   If ....

2. Travelling on a spaceship will probably make you feel sick.
   When you ....

3. The soldiers will get to the space station too late to stop the rocket from leaving.
   By the time ....

4. I predict an economic crisis in about six months' time.
   In my opinion, ...

5. I've arranged to go to Paris next Tuesday.
   I'm ....

6. 3.25 p.m. is the time of the next train for Gatwick.
    The next train for Gatwick ....

7. We will have lunch on arrival at Houston.
    As soon as ....

8. The launch of the balloon will not take place if the weather is bad.
    Unless ....

9. Spanish is what I have decided to learn next year.
    I am ....

10. On arrival at the airport, please collect your hand-luggage.
    When you ....

Vocabulary Building   Adjectives with prepositions

Many adjectives are followed by prepositions when they are used in phrases. You can be, for example, good *at* something or frightened *of* somebody or something. It is useful to learn which prepositions commonly-used adjectives are followed by.

1. Match the adjectives below with the prepositions. Be careful! Some can be followed by more than one preposition.

    angry   aware   good   envious
    terrified   furious   frightened   bad
            at   about   of   with
    happy   worried   anxious   scared
        afraid   impatient   jealous

2. Most of the above adjectives describe 'feelings'. Which three adjectives do not?

3. Turn the adjectives of 'feeling' into nouns, and then make sentences which describe when you have these feelings. For example:

    Anger is a feeling I have when someone stops me doing what I want.

Extension   'Come to the Moon for a better life!'

Look at this brochure telling people about life in Milton Keynes, a new town. What do the people who have written the brochure think will appeal to people? Why will they lead a better life in Milton Keynes?

MILTON KEYNES

— fastest growing city in Britain —

TRANSPORT   Milton Keynes is within easy reach of most of the country. The M1 Motorway runs past the city, and the main London to Glasgow railway line has a station here. The main roads inside the City are arranged on a simple grid pattern — so you can't get lost. And there is ample parking for everyone!

BUSINESS   Many international companies have offices here, ranging from Coca-Cola to Mercedes Benz. There is low unemployment and many new jobs are created every year. Employment areas are placed around the City to avoid the traditional rush-hour traffic jams.

RECREATION   Milton Keynes has three Leisure Centres offering a wide range of sports facilities. There are many cinemas, an ice-rink, an Arts Centre, several health and fitness clubs. And of course there are water sports on Willen Lake.

PARKLAND   We call Milton Keynes 'the city of trees'. 10 million trees and shrubs have been planted here to date. There are over 4,000 acres of parkland, a bird sanctuary, and, for the less energetic, there are many shorter walks along the canal.

Now imagine that you are a member of the Moon Settlement Committee. You have to get as many people as possible to come and live on the Moon.

Unfortunately people are not very interested, and so you have decided that you should write a brochure to persuade people that the Moon is a good place to live and to advertise the benefits of living on the Moon. Tell them in this brochure what their future lives will be like.

Make sentences like:

On the Moon you will get away from the noise of the big cities.

UNIT FIVE

LEISURE

Foundations

1. Look at the leisure activities shown in the photos. Can you name them?

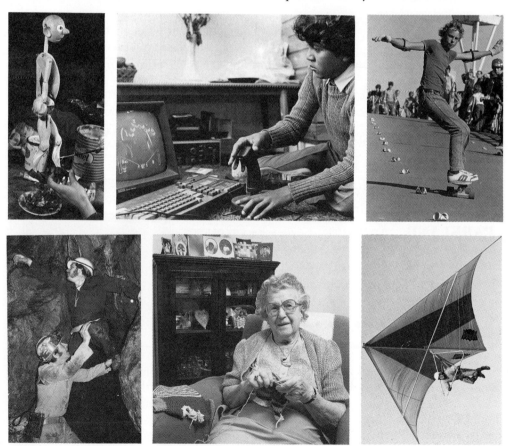

2. In pairs or small groups, list all the leisure activities you do. Compare your list with the other groups.

3. If you could take up one new activity, what would it be? Try to imagine the 'best moment' in this new activity and then write a sentence or two describing this moment. For example, someone who chooses mountaineering might write:

The best moment for me would be when I was at the top of a mountain that I had just climbed. I would feel tired and proud, and I would have a fantastic view that few people had seen before.

Then read out your sentence and see if your partner, or the rest of the class, can guess what your activity would be.

4. Read the passage below quickly so that you can answer the following question. Do not try to fill in the blanks yet.

The people in this passage are on holiday in Africa. Which of these activities are they doing?

a Hunting lions
b Looking for wild animals
c Studying vultures

Before our first outing, the leader of the camp gave us a brief talk. 'If anything alarming .... (1),' he said, 'don't, on any account, run away. There is a man with a gun to defend .... (2) and you just need to do exactly .... (3) I say.'

We kept .... (4) advice in mind on our expeditions.

One .... (5) there was a wonderful howling and screaming of hyenas, followed .... (6) a great roaring of lions. .... (7) the morning we saw a group of vultures .... (8) than a mile away, and our leader thought that we .... (9) investigate in case they were gathering over a dead .... (10).

We set out and, before going very far, we found the body of a buffalo .... (11) had obviously been killed the night .... (12). Our leader, who was interested .... (13) lions, said the lion must still .... (14) very near, because the vultures .... (15) waiting in the nearby trees, and not eating the body. He was soon proved right: we just managed to .... (16) sight of a golden back disappearing behind .... (17) bushes.

Most of our walking was less alarming than .... (18). We walked .... (19) day and, ... (20) we wanted, drove by night with a spotlight.

5. In pairs or small groups, find a suitable title for the passage.

6. Read the passage again and complete blanks (1)–(10) only.

7. Look at blank number (5) again. What did you write? There are at least two possibilities, and you can only find out which one is correct by looking carefully at the sentence which follows it.

8. Now complete blanks (11)–(20).

9. Refer to the passage to fill in the boxes below.

ALL THE ANIMALS MENTIONED	ALL THE ANIMAL NOISES MENTIONED

Can you add to the boxes by writing in as many animals and their noises as you can think of?

Extension   'Adventure!'

KATHMANDU: 3 young people needed to join a team of 8 journeying overland by Landrover to Nepal. Will visit major cities on the way. Starting from London in early August. Time is not a problem. The adventure of a lifetime! Apply with personal details to Box 302.

AMAZON ADVENTURE

A group of young people will be leaving home for the first time this summer — and will go straight into the jungle! The Royal Geographical Association is paying for up to 20 people, aged between 16 and 21, to join a study trip which will visit five small villages in the Amazonian jungle. The idea is for them to come back with new ideas about life in developing societies — but we will be pleased if they come back alive. There are still five places free. So if anyone is brave enough to go, they had better apply soon.

PONYTREKKING IN WALES

Get to see the famous mountains of Wales, and hardly walk a step! Let our ponies carry you and your camping equipment while you enjoy the fantastic views. There will be swimming in the rivers by day, and singing round the camp fires by night. *Come pony-trekking with us, any time from June until September.*

Above are advertisements for three adventure holidays. Imagine that you and a group of friends can go on one of these holidays. In pairs or small groups, choose which holiday you will go on, and then make the following decisions:

a How long will you go for?
b What will you take with you? (Make a list of equipment, provisions, etc.)
c Will you try to raise money to help pay for the holiday? How might you do this?

Now compare your answers with other groups.

Exam Training   Letter expansion questions

In the *Use of English* paper you are required to do either a letter expansion question or a dialogue completion question. We will look at letter expansion questions in this unit and at dialogue completions in Unit 6.

What you need to know

The exam instructions: *Make all the changes and additions necessary to produce, from the following sets of words and phrases, sentences which together make a complete letter. Note carefully from the example what kind of alterations need to be made. Write each sentence in the space provided.*

EXAMPLE: I be very surprised/receive/letter/you this morning.
ANSWER: *I was very surprised to receive a letter from you this morning.*

1. Look at the letter expansion exercise below so that you can answer the following questions:
    – How many sentences are there to complete?
    – What do the bars (/) in the exercise mean?
    – What do you have to do when there is a bar?

    Dear Sally and Jim,
    As you see/stamp/letter/we be/holiday in Malta.
    a) ....
    We stay/beautiful hotel/magnificent swimming pool.
    b) ....
    Since we arrive/spend nearly/day on/beach,/be near our hotel.
    c) ....

Yesterday, though, we decide/do something different/we hire/boat/go sailing.
d)...

Tomorrow and the next day we hire/car/have a look around/rest/island.
e)...

After/we come back here/another week.
f)...

The food be very good/lots/seafood and fresh fish/we often eat outdoors/
swimming pool.
g)...

I know/be much healthier for us/go/walking holiday like your brother suggest
but we can do/next year.
h)...

       See you soon. Look after yourselves.

       Love,

2.   Now look at the exercise as it should be completed, below, and underline all
the words which have been added. Then answer the following questions:
  – How many words can be added at any one point?
  – What kinds of words have been added? Can you find examples of:

Nouns	....	Pronouns	....
Adverbs	....	Conjunctions	....
Verbs	....	Prepositions	....
Articles	....		

  – What form are most of the verbs written in? What do you have to do with
them?

Dear Sally and Jim,

a) As you WILL/CAN see FROM THE stamp ON THE/THIS letter we ARE
ON holiday in Malta.
b) We ARE STAYING IN/AT A beautiful hotel WITH A/WHICH HAS A
magnificent swimming pool.
c) Since we ARRIVED WE HAVE SPENT nearly EVERY day on THE beach,
WHICH IS near our hotel.
d) Yesterday, though, we DECIDED TO do something different SO/AND we
HIRED A boat AND WENT/TO GO sailing.
e) Tomorrow and the next day we WILL/ARE GOING TO hire A car
AND/TO have a look around THE rest OF THE island.
f) After THAT we WILL COME back here FOR another week.
g) The food IS very good WITH lots OF seafood and fresh fish AND we
often eat outdoors NEAR THE/BESIDE THE swimming pool.

h) I know IT WOULD HAVE BEEN much healthier for us TO go ON/FOR A walking holiday like your brother SUGGESTED but we can do THAT next year.

See you soon. Look after yourselves.

Love,

How to prepare

You will now have noticed that you do not need to add any new information to the letter. The most important part of your job is to decide what verb forms to use: you have to ask yourself if each sentence is describing something in the past, present or future. You will not be able to answer this without understanding the **context** of the letter.

For this reason, as with the blank-filling exercise in Unit 1, always read the exercise to the end before trying to answer it. And ask yourself the following questions:

- What is the relationship between the writer and receiver of the letter?
- Why is the writer sending the letter?
- Which events in the letter are past, which present and which future?

NOTE: you should always be looking for expressions of time, e.g. *yesterday, last week, now*, etc.

3.   Look at the following letter expansion question and answer the above three questions.

Dear Aunt Jill

It be lovely/see you last week.

a) ....

I be sorry I have/rush/catch/last train and we couldn't talk/longer.

b) ....

I like/thank you/invite me/play/Theatre Royal,/I really enjoy.

c) ....

I always love Shakespeare,/it be wonderful/see/production/one of his most famous plays.

d) ....

I be sure it help me/my English exams,/I take next month.

e) ....

I write you/longer letter/all/exams be over.

f) ....

We also like/come/visit you when/weather get better.

g) ....

Thank/very/once again/everything.

h) ....

Love,   Mary

4. Now complete the letter.

How to practise

5. Read this final letter expansion exercise and
   - remind yourself of what kinds of words you are looking for, as you did in 2.
   - answer the questions about the context, as you did in 3.
   - look for any expressions of time
   - complete the exercise

Dear Sir,

I write/complain/the service/Dizzy Castle Leisure Centre,/I go/my three children yesterday.

a) ....

First, we have/wait/two hours/get in/only one entrance be open.

b) ....

Then, there be such long queues/be impossible/us/go on anything.

c) ....

After/while we all need/ice-cream/ice-cream shop be closed.

d) ....

We buy/sandwiches instead/they be/disgusting we throw/away.

e) ....

By then we be so angry/upset/decide/go home.

f) ....

We certainly/not visit Dizzy Castle again.

g) ....

Yours faithfully,

Peter Martin

Extension   'On safari . . .'

The Wingate Wildlife Park, advertised below, only opened a month ago. There are still many attractions and facilities it does not yet offer.

Read through the information about the park, and then, in pairs or small groups, decide what you would do to improve it.

Wingate Wild Life Park
A DAY OUT FOR ALL THE FAMILY

*Wingate **Wild L**ife **P**ark houses a large and varied collection of animals from all over the world. Wherever possible deep moats are used instead of high fences, so there is nothing to obstruct your view of the animals.*

ANIMALS There are wild animals in the spacious, grassed enclosures, including tigers, leopards, rhinos, zebras and many others. But also, for younger children, there are farm animals that they can get closer to, such as sheep, cows, goats, etc.

GARDENS We are very proud of the new garden development. There is now a large variety of named trees and shrubs, and also extensive lawns which can be used for picnics.

RESTAURANT There is a restaurant offering full self-service facilities. Reduced meal prices for large parties are available on request.

PLAYGROUND A new adventure playground is being built near the restaurant. It is also possible for you to bring and eat your own picnics in this area.

Grammar Building   Infinitive or the-*ing* form

1. Look at the following three lists of verbs. The lists are of:

> verbs + infinitive with *to*
> verbs + -*ing* form
> verbs + either form

The lists do not include every verb in each category but do include the most common ones. Look at the lists and write the correct heading at the top of each list.

VERB + ...	VERB + ...	VERB + ...
afford	allow*	avoid
agree	attempt	consider
appear	can't bear	delay
arrange	begin	deny
ask	continue	dislike
choose	fear	enjoy
decide	feel*	finish
expect	forget*	give up
fail	hate	can't help/stand
help	hear*	imagine
hope	intend	keep
learn	like	mind
manage	love	miss
offer	mean*	practise
plan	prefer	risk
prepare	regret*	suggest
pretend	remember*	
promise	see*	
refuse	start	
seem	stop*	
want	watch*	
wish		

verbs with* change their meaning depending on which form is used

2. Read the following newspaper article about a group of old people's leisure activities and work out the correct form of the verb.

> **Where life begins at eighty!**
> Most afternoons at Happy Valley old people's home the fifty or so residents enjoy [1](play) a game of bingo.
>   John Smith is typical of many of the pensioners at the home whose motto seems [2](be) 'Life begins at eighty!'
>   'We keep busy all the time,' he says. 'Jan, who is the supervisor of the

home, encourages us all ³(do) all kinds of activities. I practise ⁴(play)
bowls. I can't imagine ⁵(sit) all day long and ⁶(do) nothing. I remember
⁷(have) lots of hobbies when I was younger and I don't intend ⁸(stop)
now.

 'I can't stand ⁹(feel) bored and I really enjoy ¹⁰(do) the classes. I plan
¹¹(study) French next because I want ¹²(go) to France for a holiday.'

 John is typical of all the residents at Happy Valley. They manage
¹³(do) a great variety of activities – from wine-making to embroidery. As
John says 'You are as young as you feel and I expect ¹⁴(stay) active for a
long time yet!'

3. Some verbs are followed by either the infinitive or the *-ing* form depending on
their meaning. Read the following passage and put the verbs in brackets into
the infinitive or the *-ing* form.

Packing for a holiday
Mary: David! Come and help me! David! David!
David: All right. Stop ¹(shout)! I'm coming.
Mary: I can't close the suitcase. There's too much in it.
David: Try ²(sit) on it. That sometimes works.
Mary: That's better. Now it's closed.
David: Did you remember ³(put) your toothbrush in?
Mary: I don't know. I remember ⁴(pick) it up, but I don't remember ⁵(put)
         it in the suitcase.
David: You're hopeless! You never remember anything!
Mary: You're no better than me! I bet you forgot ⁶(collect) the tickets from
         the travel agent.
David: No, I remembered ⁷(get) them. I stopped ⁸(collect) them on my way
         back from work, but I don't know where I put them. Didn't I put
         them in your handbag?
Mary: I didn't see you ⁹(put) them in my handbag.
David: Listen! I think I heard a car ¹⁰(stop) outside the house.
Mary: It's the taxi.
David: But I haven't found the tickets!
Mary: Stop ¹¹(worry)! Just try ¹²(remember) what you did with them. Try
         ¹³(look) in your pockets.
David: Here they are! How did they get there? I had quite forgotten ¹⁴(put)
         them there.

Extension   A Character Test

You are going to make a questionnaire to test your character, or the character of
your friends. Below are some statements which you must write out in full and then
say if you agree or disagree with them.

First, write out the statements in full. You will have to decide whether to use the infinitive form or the *-ing* form.

Secondly, draw five small boxes at the end of each statement and put the following numbers into them: $\boxed{+2 \mid +1 \mid 0 \mid -1 \mid -2}$ You will then mark one of these numbers for each statement and, at the end, add up your total score.

This is what the numbers mean:

+2	means	agree strongly
+1	means	agree
0	means	have no feelings about it
−1	means	disagree
−2	means	disagree strongly

NOTE: Some people may have a minus score, e.g. −10, some may have a plus score, e.g. +10, and some may even score 0. What do these scores say about your character?

1. If I enjoy (do) something which other people say is bad for me, I do it anyway.
2. If I can't do something, I practise (do) it until I am good at it.
3. If people wish (be) happy, they have to risk (be) unhappy.
4. If someone tells me (do) something I don't like, I simply refuse (do) it.
5. If someone tells me (do) something I don't like, I simply forget (do) it.
6. People who can't bear (be) poor should plan (be) rich.
7. If I decide (do) something, I must not fail (do) it.
8. I should never regret (do) what I intended (do).
9. I can usually afford (buy) what I want, because I can usually borrow the money.
10. People who delay (do) difficult things are really trying to avoid (do) them.

Now compare your answers with the rest of the class.

Revision Transformations

Finish each of the following sentences in such a way that it means exactly the same as the sentence printed before it.

1. 'Why don't we go windsurfing tomorrow?' John said.
    John suggested ....

2. Toshi's skis still hadn't been cleaned.
    Toshi's skis still needed ....

3. The gambler said that he had not cheated at cards.
    The gambler denied ....

4. It annoys me when people smoke in restaurants.
    I can't stand people ....

5. We couldn't swim in the sea because of strong currents.
   Strong currents stopped ....

6. Did I pay the bill? I don't remember.
   I don't remember ....

7. His boss told him he couldn't go home early.
   His boss wouldn't allow ....

8. 'Go to the cinema!' Anne said.
   Anne encouraged us ....

9. Oh, yes. I'm certain I saw a football match.
   I remember ....

10. Jason never hits the ball.
    Jason keeps ....

Vocabulary Building

Word Sets

In five minutes, write down all the words you can think of belonging to the four groups below:

CINEMA	HOBBIES	HOLIDAYS	SPORTS

Compare your list with three or four other people's and add any extra words to your list.

Word Building

Use the word endings below to make as many words as possible. The spelling of some words will need to change.

WORD	ENDING
amuse	-able
delight	-ful
enjoy	-ing
entertain	-ment
like	

Compare your list with a partner's or your dictionary. What kind of feeling do all these words show?

List the things that you do in your leisure time which you would use these words to describe.

Extension   'A weekend in London'

Imagine you have just arrived in London for a short weekend visit. In pairs or small groups, plan your weekend taking into account all your interests and hobbies. Write your decisions in the table below.

London Zoo

London Zoo, Regent's Park, NW1
(722 3333) Open daily 9 a.m.–6 p.m.
Children £2; adults £3.90

Meet the Animals is a twice daily show in the Hummingbird Amphitheatre. A talk by the keepers is followed by a chance to meet and stroke the animals which vary from day to day but might include a camel, a baby chimpanzee, a penguin or a parrot. *Feeding sessions* are at 12 noon for the fish, 1.30 p.m. for the pelicans, 2 p.m. for the penguins and 3.30 p.m. for the sea-lions. *Animal rides* including camels, donkeys, ponies, and llama and pony carts, are available daily from 1.30 p.m.

DAYTIME ACTIVITIES

London Dungeon 28 Tooley St, SE1 (403 0606) London Bridge tube. Daily 10am-5.30pm. Under 14s £2, adults £3.50. Exhibition depicting the darker side of British history – death, torture and disease. Pretty gory but older kids love it.

Museum of Mankind Burlington Gardens, W1 (437 2224) Picadilly / Green Park tube. Mon.–Sat. 10 a.m.–5 p.m., Sun. 2.30–6 p.m. Adm. free. Regularly changing exhibitions illustrate aspects of non-Western societies and cultures. The current major exhibition, *Living Arctic* paints a detailed and fascinating picture of the contemporary lifestyle and history of the Indian and Inuit people of the Canadian North.

Planetarium Marylebone Rd, NW1 (486 1121) Baker Street tube. Shows every 40 mins Children £1.40, Adults £2.20. Combined ticket including entrance to Madame Tussaud's: Children £3.10, Adult £5.15. *Starburst* uses the most recent technology and information to tell the story of stars from birth to explosive extinction. You can combine your trip with a visit to Madame Tussaud's next door. Enter via the Planetarium — the queues are shorter.

Circus Skills Every Sat. 10.30 a.m.–12.30 p.m. Watermans Arts Centre, 40 High St., Brentford. South Ealing / Gunnersbury tube. Tumbling, juggling, tightrope walking, unicycling and clowning for 9 to 15 year-olds. £3. Early booking recommended.

Coram's Fields family workshops Every Sat 2.30–5 p.m. 93 Guildford St., WC1. Russell Square tube. Try your hand at making raku pots, build a huge model car or make a stuffed dinosaur. Details from the Mary Ward Centre on 831 7711.

FILMS

CANNON, Panton St, SW1
Hope and Glory   This is a film about the bombing of London during the war as seen through the eyes of a nine-year-old boy.
Times: 2.20, 4.50, 7.25

CANNON, Piccadilly
White Mischief   A story of lies and murder among the rich whites in Kenya. The cast includes Greta Scacchi, Charles Dance and John Hurt.
Times: 3.40, 6.00, 8.20 Late Sat. 11.15

EMPIRE, Leicester Sq.
Cry Freedom   The film tells how the white editor of a newspaper in South Africa is won over by the black leader, Steve Biko. After Biko's murder by the police, the editor finds life in South Africa difficult and very dangerous.
Times: 3.00, 6.00, 9.00 Late Sat. 11.55

WARNER, Leicester Sq.
Three Men and a Baby   Three young men who share a flat find a baby on their doorstep one morning. They try to look after it, but things start to go wrong very quickly
Times: 1.55, 4.10, 6.25, 8.45

	SATURDAY	SUNDAY
morning		
afternoon		
evening		

UNIT SIX

HEALTH

Foundations

1. Write the words for the parts of the body which are labelled in the picture below.

2. Now use these words to label the picture below: appendix, heart, intestines, kidneys, liver, lungs, stomach.

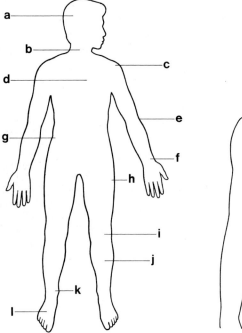

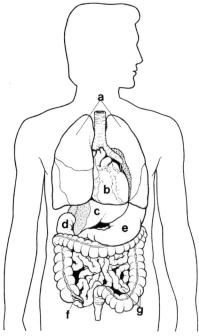

3. In pairs or small groups, list at least twelve health or medical problems you can have in different parts of the body.

4. Read the passage below quickly so that you can answer the following questions. Do not try to fill in the blanks yet.

   a What does the first paragraph tell us about the origins of acupuncture?
   b Who was Pien Chueh?

   According to an ancient Chinese legend, the idea of acupuncture* began when a man developed a headache while lifting some heavy rocks. The headache was .... (1) severe that he dropped .... (2) of the rocks .... (3) his foot. His foot became very painful and .... (4) to bleed. .... (5) his headache stopped. From this the practice of acupuncture developed, although the rock .... (6) replaced by a variety of needles. The first acupuncture needles were .... (7) of stone, bone, bamboo, copper, iron or silver, but today stainless steel is usually used.

   You can read an early description of acupuncture treatment in the 'Biographies of Pien Chueh and Tsang Kung' which was written over two thousand years .... (8). Pien Chueh was famous .... (9) his skill in acupuncture, massage and the use of herbal medicines. One day he was with his two assistants in an area called Kuo .... (10) he heard that the Prince of Kuo was very seriously .... (11). When Pien Chueh arrived at the palace, preparations .... (12) the Prince's funeral were already .... (13) made. Pien Chueh examined the Prince and .... (14) he was still breathing, but only weakly. He immediately ordered .... (15) of his assistants to treat him with acupuncture, while the .... (16) assistant placed bunches of special herbs in his armpits. Soon the Prince recovered consciousness and was .... (17) to sit .... (18) in bed. Pien Chueh recommended that he should .... (19) certain herbal medicines for twenty days. The Prince .... (20) this and was soon fit and healthy again.

   *That is, treating an illness in one part of the body by pricking another part of the body with a needle.

5. Which of the following is the most suitable title for the passage:

   a The Story of Pien Chueh
   b The Story of the Prince of Kuo
   c The Story of Acupuncture

6. Read the passage again and complete the blanks.

7. Look at blank number (11) again. How did you find the answer? Were you helped by the sentence before, or by the sentence after?

8. Make a list of all the words in the passage related to the topic of health (including ill-health).

Extension   'Doctor, doctor . . .'

Imagine that you are Pien Chueh. A woman has had an accident and needs to have an operation urgently. Before you can give her the operation, however, there are four things that you must put right to prepare her for the operation:

1 She has a high temperature – you cannot operate until her temperature comes down.
2 She is very weak – she needs to be stronger before you can operate.
3 She has low blood pressure – it is very dangerous to operate on her while her blood pressure is low.
4 You must stop her from feeling the pain of the operation.

You have five ways of treating her to prepare her for the operation. Some will help her, and some won't. You can use as many of them as you like, but you may have to use them in the correct order. There is only one correct solution to this problem. Below is a list of the five ways and of their effects:

a **Eating**

increases her blood pressure
increases her temperature
makes her stronger

b **Leeches**
(small animals which
suck blood; place
them on the patient's
skin)

decrease her blood pressure
decrease her temperature

c **Herb A**
(to be given as a drink)

stops her feeling pain
decreases her temperature
has no effect if she has been eating

d **Herb B**
(to be given as a drink)

decreases her temperature
makes her lose her appetite

e **Acupuncture**

stops her feeling pain

In pairs or small groups, decide what treatment you would give her (and in what order) to prepare her for the operation. Explain your treatment to the other groups.

Exam Training   Dialogue completion questions

In the *Use of English* paper you are required to do either a letter expansion question or a dialogue completion question. This section will look at dialogue completion questions. Letter expansions questions are practised in Unit 5.

What you need to know

The exam instructions: *John is telephoning his sister, Mary, about a party they are preparing for their mother's 50th birthday. Fill in the parts of the dialogue, numbered (1) to (7), which have been left blank.*

or

Helen Hampton, a famous actress, has just arrived in New York. She is being interviewed on television. Fill in the parts of the interview, numbered (1) to (7), which have been left blank.

As you can see, the exam instructions give you the **context** of the dialogue. You will still need to read through the whole passage before completing the dialogue, but you will have a clear idea of what it is about straight away.

1. Now look at this example of a dialogue completion question. What can you say about the kinds of sentences you will have to write? Do not complete the blank sentences yet.

   Mr Woods is visiting his doctor. Fill in the parts of the dialogue, numbered (1) to (6), which have been left blank.

Mr Woods:	Doctor, I'm not feeling very well.
Doctor:	What (1) ....?
Mr Woods:	I've got this awful pain. It's here – in my stomach.
Doctor:	Just how (2) ....?
Mr Woods:	About a month.
Doctor:	Do you (3) ....?
Mr Woods:	No, I usually get it after I have eaten.
Doctor:	What (4) ....?
Mr Woods:	It's difficult to say. A sort of stabbing pain, like a knife. It comes and goes.
Doctor:	Have you (5)...?
Mr Woods:	No, never. This is the first time.
Doctor:	What (6) ....?
Mr Woods:	The same as everyone else – meat, potatoes, vegetables. Things like that.
Doctor:	OK then, Mr Woods, I'd just like to examine you.
Mr Woods:	OK, Doctor.

   There are four things you should be able to notice from the above passage:

   a You are given at least the first word of the sentences that you must complete.

   b The sentences that you must complete are very often, but not always, questions.

c The sentence that comes **after** the blank is the one which gives you the most information about how to complete the sentence (although you should always look at the sentence before as well).

d The examiners try to avoid giving you too much help, i.e. they don't generally give you answers that you can simply turn into questions. Look especially at number (6) above for an example of this.

2. In pairs or small groups, complete the missing sentences. Then read the complete dialogue aloud, taking it in turns to be the doctor and Mr Woods.

How to prepare

Forming questions correctly is a very important part of dialogue completion questions. You must decide what type of question is needed, what tense is needed and how the question is formed in English. There are basically two types of question:

- questions you can answer with *yes* or *no*, e.g. Is it cold? Can you hear me? etc. These questions begin with auxiliary verbs (*have, do, will, can, should,* etc.)
- questions that need more information – these questions begin with words like *what, who, why, when, how,* etc.

The examiner gives you the first word of the question, so you should already know what kind of question is needed. All you need to do is to work out from the answer what the question is about.

3. Below are ten answers. Write suitable questions for them. In this exercise, unlike the exam, you will not be given the first word to help you.

a .... ?
    £1.50 a kilo.

b .... ?
    Since I was a child.

c .... ?
    Oh, I've already seen it. Why don't we go to a restaurant instead?

d .... ?
    No, it's raining.

e .... ?
    He's very nice.

f .... ?
    Yes, of course, Madam, which size?

g .... ?
    In February probably – there's bound to be snow.

h .... ?
    Three – two boys and a girl.

i .... ?
    Yes, there's a good programme on at 10 o'clock which I want to see.

j .... ?
    Yes, it's just gone half past ten.

4. Take a piece of paper and cut it in two. On one half write down four questions; on the other half write down the answers to your questions. Give the answers only to a partner. When your partner has written suitable questions for them, he or she must read out the questions and you will read out the answers.

How to practise

In the dialogue completion questions you must be careful to use language that suits the type of situation. You need to decide if the situation is formal, neutral or informal and choose your language accordingly.

5. Look at these two dialogues. One is an informal situation; the other is a more formal situation. Can you point to any words or phrases in the two dialogues which show the difference?

Two friends on the phone:	*Two businessmen on the phone:*
A 927 3261	A 924 3263. Edward Brown speaking.
B	B ....
A Hi, how are you?	A Oh, good morning. How are you?
B ....?	B ....?
A Fine.	A Very well, thank you.
B ....?	B ....?
A Yes, that would be great.	A How very kind. I'd love to.
B	B ....
A OK. Eight o'clock at your place.	A So, eight o'clock at your house.
B	B ....
A See you. Bye!	A I'll look forward to seeing you this evening. Goodbye.

Now complete the above dialogues using a suitable level of formality for your answers.

In pairs, read the dialogues aloud taking it in turns to be A and B in both dialogues. Feel the difference in relationships that the language reflects.

6. Now practise an exercise on your own. Remember to read the instructions carefully so that you understand the context, and read through the whole passage before you start. Think about which tenses you are going to use, and look out for any expressions of time which might help you.

A doctor is being interviewed on a radio programe about aromatherapy, a method of treating people who are stressed or depressed. Fill in the parts of the interview, numbered (1) to (6), which have been left blank.

Interviewer: Dr Bell, we're very pleased you can be with us here tonight.
Dr Bell: I'm pleased to be here.
Interviewer: Tell us (1).. .
Dr Bell: Aromatherapy is the use of flower and plant oils to treat or prevent disease.
Interviewer: And what (2) .... ?
Dr Bell: It's used particularly to treat stress and also to prevent infections.
Interviewer: How (3) .... ?
Dr Bell: You can make them into a drink or rub them into your skin.
Interviewer: Who (4) .... ?
Dr Bell: Aromatherapy was started about fifty years ago by the French doctor, René Gallefossé, but it goes back a long time before that. We know for example, that the ancient Egyptians and Chinese used plant oils.
Interviewer: And what (5) .... ?
Dr Bell: They used them to cure diseases and also to help people relax.
Interviewer: So does (6) .... ?
Dr Bell: Oh, yes, definitely. Aromatherapy can be very useful in reducing stress and tension.
Interviewer: Well, Doctor, I'm afraid that's all we've got time for today. Thank you very much for explaining this interesting treatment.

Grammar Building   Passive; *have (something) done*

Passive

1. Read this Problem Page taken from a magazine and then complete the table below in note form.

Baldness

Dear Helen,
I've heard about a new drug from America which is used to treat baldness. Does it work and where can I buy it?
Yours,
George Thompson

Helen: The drug you're talking about – Brandex – isn't in fact a new drug. It has been sold for a number of years in tablet form as a treatment for high blood pressure. Its effect on hair growth was discovered accidentally when some patients using it for their blood pressure started to regrow hair they'd previously lost.

Since then it has been shown that if Brandex is applied to the scalp in liquid form, some – but not all – people will begin to grow their hair again.

Itching and skin disease can be caused by Brandex and it is not recommended for use by elderly people.

Colour Blind

Dear Helen,
I think my three-year-old son might be colour blind. How can I find out for sure?
Yours sincerely,
Marjorie Troops

Helen: Colour blindness affects about eight in 100 boys and one in 200 girls. The most common difficulty is in telling the difference between red and green. Young children may confuse the names given to colours and so may appear colour blind when in fact they're not. True colour blindness can be easily detected by your doctor using special colour cards. If your son is colour blind you should make sure that teachers know about the problem when he starts school, because colour codes are often used in teaching.

	ENQUIRER'S PROBLEM	DOCTOR'S ADVICE
Mr Thompson		
Mrs Troops		

2. Read the Problem Page again and underline the verbs in the passive. How many examples of modal verbs used with a passive infinitive can you find?

3. Read the following two reports of an accident. If you were the manager of the laundry, which one would you use to tell the customer about the accident?

   a When you brought the silk dress in, we put the wrong label on it. We put the dress into the wrong machine, and boiled it. We ruined your dress.

   b When the silk dress was brought in, it was incorrectly labelled. The dress was placed in the wrong machine, and was cleaned at a very high temperature. The dress has been damaged beyond repair.

   What language differences did you notice?

4. Look at the following sentences. They are all good English, but some are in the active and some are in the passive.
   What differences of meaning do you notice? Use these differences to find a suitable context for each sentence. Try to think who is saying it, and why they are using the active or the passive.

   a There are some people who think that this drug helps to reduce heart attacks.
   It is thought that this drug helps to reduce heart attacks.

   b We can't diagnose your illness.
   Your illness cannot be diagnosed.

   c Someone in this room has robbed me!
   I've been robbed!

   d This room must be cleaned.
   You must clean this room.

   e We can do nothing.
   Nothing can be done.

   f No smoking.
   Please don't smoke.
   Smoking is forbidden.
   Customers are requested not to smoke.

5. Can you think of any more situations where we use the passive (or the passive is used) in a similar way?

6. Complete these sentences by putting the verb in brackets into the correct form of the passive. Some sentences may also need modal verbs.

   a Many illnesses .... with penicillin.   (TREAT)
   b Antibiotics .... earlier this century.   (DISCOVER)
   c Many drugs .... by pregnant women.   (NOT TAKE)
   d Colds .... by taking lots of vitamin C.   (PREVENT)

e I hope that one day a cure for Aids ....   (FIND)
f Alcohol .... by young children.   (NOT DRINK)
g Radiation .... to treat cancer.   (USE)
h It .... some forms of exercise are bad for you.   (SAY)

Have (something) done

7. Look at this list of things that need to be done. Say which of them you can do for yourself, and which of them need to be done for you. For example:

    I have/get my blood pressure checked (by a doctor).
    but
    I brush my hair myself.

    Wash your hair   Measure your height
    Cut your hair   Dye your hair
    Brush your teeth   Check your teeth
    Test your eyes   Take your pulse
    Take your temperature   Take your appendix out
    X-ray your chest   Cut your nails

Revision Transformations

Finish each of the following sentences in such a way that it means exactly the same as the sentence printed before it.

1. They drew up plans to build a large new hospital three years ago.
    Plans ....

2. The school gym still needs painting.
    The school gym hasn't ....

3. John had his eyes tested last week.
    John's eyes ....

4. It is essential for us to reduce the amount of sugar we eat.
    The amount of sugar we eat ....

5. Scientists have still not found a cure for cancer.
    A cure for cancer ....

6. A woman in a green hat showed me the way to the hospital.
    I ....

7. A lot of people say that sugar is bad for you.
    Sugar ....

8. The doctor advised Felicity to give up smoking immediately.
    Felicity ....

9. We need to exercise all our muscles regularly if we want to stay fit.
    All our muscles ....

10. The dentist checks my teeth every six months.
    I have ....

Vocabulary Building   Word Sets; phrasal verbs; word building

Word Sets

A useful way to build up your vocabulary is to have a 'brainstorm' and write down as many words on a topic as you can think of.

1. In pairs, and without looking back through the unit, write down as many words as you can about Health in five minutes. A few have been done to start you off. Compare your diagram of words with some other pairs'. Add any words you did not think of to your list.

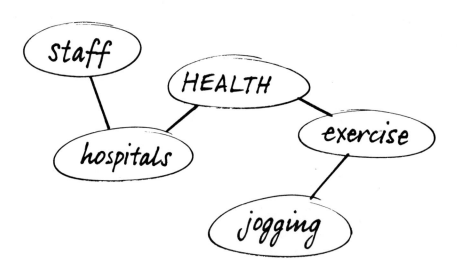

Phrasal Verbs

Many verbs are regularly found with particular nouns when you are talking about specific situations, for example the word *check-up* is found most commonly with the verbs *go for* or *have*.

2. Match the phrasal verbs in the left-hand column with a noun in the right-hand column. One has been done for you. NOTE: Some nouns may go with more than one verb.

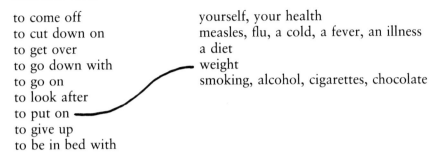

to come off   yourself, your health
to cut down on   measles, flu, a cold, a fever, an illness
to get over   a diet
to go down with   weight
to go on   smoking, alcohol, cigarettes, chocolate
to look after
to put on
to give up
to be in bed with

Word Building

3. Use the word beginnings and/or endings below to make at least twelve new words. The spellings of some words will need to change.

    For example: clean ⟶ cleanly ⟶ cleanliness.

BEGINNING	WORD	ENDING
in-	clean	-able
un-	digest	-cy
	efficient	-ful
	pain	-ion
	safe	-ive
		-ly
		-less
		-ness
		-ty

4. Now in groups use at least ten of these words to continue the following story. You can use a word more than once if you wish.

    Last summer Uncle George got a terrible pain in his stomach. He thought it was just indigestion, but his wife . . .

    Compare your stories. Whose was the most interesting?

Extension   'An apple a day keeps the doctor away!'

In pairs or small groups, decide on the best health advertising slogans for each of the items on the next page. When you have made your slogans, read them out to the rest of the class and decide which is the best for each item.

Slimming: *Before...*

...and after!

HEALTH INSURANCE

You never know when you are going to be ill, or when you are going to have an accident. It often happens at the very worst of times. You can't go to work, and so the money stops coming in. And that's when the hospital bills start to come instead.

With private health insurance, you know that when things go wrong you can get them right again quickly.

UNIT SEVEN

EDUCATION

Foundations

1. Look at these photos and then note down all the words and phrases that come into your mind when you think of your own education.

2. Put these words into a suitable section below.

cheating   report   bored   gym   playground
homework   history   chemistry   sports   boring
classroom   library   biology   intelligent lazy
careless   maths   art   tests   exam
continuous assessment hard-working literature interesting science lab
essay

THINGS YOU DO AT SCHOOL	TYPES OF ASSESSMENT	PLACES AT SCHOOL	DESCRIPTIONS OF PEOPLE

3.   Add at least three other words you know to each of these categories. Compare your list with a partner's and add any different ones to your list.

4.   What do you think helps people to learn? Put (1) by the most important, (2) by the next most important, and so on.

parents	sports
school uniform	good health
good school equipment	play
correct diet	good weather
sleep	condition of the classroom (temperature,
books	lighting etc.)

Discuss your answers. Do you agree with each other? Explain why you have put the choices in a particular order.

5.   Read the passage below quickly so that you can answer the following questions. Do not try to fill in the blanks yet.

a   Where do you think this passage comes from: a newspaper, a magazine or a radio talk?
b   The teacher is trying to find a connection between two things. What are they?

I'm a teacher and a few years ago I started getting worried about my students because they weren't concentrating in lessons and had difficulties following what I was saying. I thought that this .... (1) perhaps because of all the fast food they eat .... (2) days. So I contacted a psychologist .... (3) a university and, with the students' and their parents' agreement, we worked out an experiment.

First of .... (4) I kept a record of everything a hundred of my students .... (5) over a three-day period and, when we analysed this record, ... (6) found that their diet did not .... (7) enough vitamins and minerals. We therefore decided to divide the students into two .... (8) and give .... (9) group vitamin pills and the other group a dummy pill .... (10) looked exactly the same .... (11) which, in fact, had no nutritional value – no vitamins or minerals at all.

The students .... (12) the pills for nine months and then we tested .... (13) to see if there was .... (14) difference in their performance. Our results showed no important differences in memory, concentration and language ability .... (15) the two groups. But the group who .... (16) taken the vitamin pills got much higher scores .... (17) the other group in tests of their mathematical ability.

I hadn't expected these findings but .... (18) does seem that what .... (19) eat influences our intelligence even when we .... (20) apparently well-fed.

6. Now choose the most suitable title for the passage:

   a Fast food is bad for you
   b Students don't concentrate in lessons
   c Students don't know what they are eating
   d What you eat changes how you think

7. What was the purpose of the teacher's experiment? Was it a good one, in your opinion? Did it prove anything?

8. Use the words below to make sentences of your own:
   concentrate   a pill
   experiment   fast food
   scores   well-fed

9. Read the passage again and complete the blanks.

Extension   'of the students, for the students, by the students'

Do you think you could improve your school? This is your chance! Your class has been elected to make changes to the whole school. You are allowed to make the following changes:
   – You may choose two new subjects and get rid of two subjects. (You may choose any subject at all!)
   – You may change one rule about what you must not do at school.
   – You may change either the time you arrive at school, or the time you leave the school, or the length of the lessons.
   – You may make one change of any kind you want.

   In pairs or small groups, decide what changes you would like to make. But, before you tell the other groups about your changes, you must elect a new headteacher. You must write a name on a piece of paper (you can choose yourself or someone else). The student with the most votes becomes the new headteacher.
   Now tell the other groups about your changes. When all the changes have been reported, the headteacher must decide which ones the school will adopt.

Exam Training   Guided writing questions (1)

1. In the *Use of English* paper you have to do a guided writing question. Look back at the guided writing question you did in the Starter Unit on page 11. What do you think this kind of question is testing? Look at the list of activities below and tick any items which you think are being tested in a guided writing question.

a reading for general information
b reading for detail
c making choices
d giving reasons for choices based on what you have read
e writing a short composition
f writing in a new form all the information contained in the texts
g understanding information presented in maps, charts, diagrams, advertisements, charts, etc.
h summarising information
i linking sentences with the correct joining words
j giving opinions

What you need to know

A guided writing question contains two main tasks:
  – finding information from a variety of texts
  – writing paragraphs in good English

  Firstly you have to look at the instructions you are given, and then find in the text or texts the information which will help you to follow those instructions.

  Secondly you have to write several paragraphs using the information you have found in the texts. To do this you need to be able to express your opinion and give good reasons for your opinion. The examiners are testing that you can:
  – understand relevant parts of the texts
  – select relevant information from the texts
  – make choices based on that information
  – explain your choices in good English

  Units 7, 8 and 9 will practise the skills you need to complete guided writing questions. This unit, and unit 8, will give you some ideas about how to find related information in different texts and how to give good reasons for your choices based on your reading.

How to prepare

In the first part of a guided writing question you have to read various texts (such as letters, advertisements, etc.). You will not need to understand every word of the texts, since you will only be asked to select information from them. This means that, to begin with, all you need to do is find out:
  – what the texts are about
  – where the different bits of information are

  There are two strategies or ways of reading that you can use to do this:

a You can **skim**. You move your eyes very quickly over the text so as to get a general idea of what the text is about, focusing on certain key words or phrases.

b You can **scan**. You look through a text for specific bits of information in the text.

When you have read the instructions, skim and scan the texts to find out what they are about and find where the information you need is.

How to practise

2.   Look at this typical example. We have taken the instructions away and left you with only the texts. Skim through the texts quickly so that you can answer these questions about them:

   a There are two kinds of texts: what different things do these texts describe?
   b There are four different classes: what are the most important differences between them?
   c What do you think the instructions will ask you to do?

Class A: 25 eleven-year-old boys and girls from the Towers Secondary School in central London. This is their first year at this school.

Class B: 15 sixteen-year-old boys who are specializing in science subjects. They attend Burtington School in outer London and like their teachers very much.

Class C: 23 seven-year-olds from St Thomas' Primary School in Reading, a town thirty miles outside London and twenty miles from Oxford.

Class D: 12 eighteen-year-old girls from Nelson School in Oxford, going on their last excursion together before going to university.

Day trips to Oxford

* Visit the beautiful university colleges
* Go rowing on the river
* See the magnificent Bodleian Library
* Visit one of Oxford's many delicious tea shops

Only one hour from London by regular express train service, or by motorway.

ONE DAY CRICKET MATCH
ENGLAND
v
NEW ZEALAND

11–6pm Lords Cricket Ground, London W8

London Natural History Museum
* special exhibitions
* reptiles through the ages
* South American butterflies
* See the 'living' dinosaurs!

All other permanent exhibitions also open. School groups welcome. Open 9–5.30 every day of the week.

London Science Museum
* the first steam engine
* an exhibition on alternative energy
* the great laser exhibition

Small classes welcome!
Open 9–5.30 Mon–Sun

Enjoy a day by the sea!
BRIGHTON
Lots to see and do!
Visit the . . .
- new yachting marina
- aquarium
- mini-golf course
- funfair
- piers
- beaches

Sixty-minute road and rail links to London;
fast trains to other cities in the south!

The Sights of Bath
* Beautiful buildings
* Enjoy a trip on the River Avon
* Visit the Roman baths – feel
  the hot water!
* Try delicious Bath buns

All this and a good train service
to London, Oxford and many other
towns in the south of England.

3. Now read the instructions that we took away from the beginning of the above
    exercise. The instructions always tell you what kind of information to look for
    in the texts. Did you guess correctly?

    *Below there is information about classes from four different schools. They
    are all planning to go on a school trip for one day and the possible trips
    are also shown below.*

    *Using the information given, decide which is the most suitable trip for each
    group, and then continue in about 50 words each of the paragraphs started
    for you below, giving your reasons.*

4. How can you decide which trip each class should choose? There is a lot of
    information, but it isn't all in the right order, and not all of it is useful. A
    good way to start is to decide what information you need.

    In 2.b (above) you looked at the differences between the classes. The best
    way to find a suitable trip for each class will be to extract these differences
    from the text so that you can see them easily.

    Below is a table that you can use to help you. Scan through the text and
    complete the table.

	TOWERS	BURTINGTON	ST THOMAS'	NELSON
SIZE OF CLASS				
AGE OF STUDENTS				
MALE/FEMALE				
TOWN				

5. Look at the chart below. A student has decided which trip she thinks each class should go on. She has written her decisions out as a table, below. Do you agree with her decisions? Are the reasons she gives based on the texts or not? If you don't agree with the choices she made, say what you would choose and why.

NAME OF SCHOOL	MOST SUITABLE TRIP	REASONS
Towers	Cricket match	class might like cricket
Burtington	Day trip to Oxford	class might like rowing and seeing colleges.
St. Thomas'	Day trip to Brighton	Seven-year-old children usually enjoy the seaside.
Nelson	Day trip to Oxford	girls going to university. They might like to celebrate leaving school in a tea-shop and rowing on the river.

Make a similar table to the one above, and then complete it with your own opinions on the most suitable trip and your reasons.

NOTE: there is often more than one suitable choice. You are not looking for a 'correct' answer, you are only looking for one or two good reasons to explain why you have made your choice.

6. In pairs or small groups, read the guided writing question below so that you can answer the following questions. Do not try to do the exam question yet.

a What are the two different kinds of text about?
b What are the most important differences between the four school governors?

St Barnabas' school has been given a sum of money and the four school governors (Mrs Green, Colonel Brown, Patricia White and Kenneth Norton) are deciding how to spend it. Some people have strong ideas about what it should be spent on. Which ideas do you think each of the governors will support, and why? Give your reasons in the spaces provided.

LOCAL SECONDARY SCHOOL HAS NO SCIENCE LABORATORY

In the twentieth century it is scandalous that a school should have no science laboratory. How can we give our children the practical education they need? How can our country plan for the future if we don't have good scientists and students who have learnt science?

TO ALL STUDENTS

Join our demonstration at 2.00 TODAY in the playground!

WE WANT A GYM!!

A healthy mind in a healthy body

To: All teachers
From: Library staff

We, the library staff, are asking for your support for a new library building. It is vital to our pupils' education that they can make use of decent library facilities. At present only 5% of our students use the library. We have an excellent range of books but nowhere to put them and nowhere to display them. Learning to read successfully is one of the most basic aims of education.

WE NEED A SCHOOL CANTEEN!
* We must be able to eat in school
* The cafés and snack bars near
  school are expensive and unhealthy
* Sandwiches are boring
* We can't all go home for lunch

HUNGRY STUDENTS DON'T LEARN WELL!

Dear Headmaster,

I recently heard about a school that sent a class on a visit to India. Although the trip was expensive, every student in that class felt that it had been the most exciting thing that they had ever done. They saw things that they had never dreamed of! Many of them said that the visit had changed their lives. The class is now organizing a project to raise money for a school they visited in Calcutta.

I know it seems extravagant, but if we sent a class to India just think of the effect it would have . . .

Mrs Green: runs a shop near the school which sells newspapers, sweets, and fruit drinks. She is thinking of making her own sandwiches to sell in the shop. She is a very keen astronomer.

Colonel Brown: used to serve with the Army in India. He thinks that everybody should take a lot of exercise, and that nobody should get anything free because it makes them lazy.

Patricia White: is a friend of Colonel Brown. She writes books for children and expects to send her daughter to St Barnabas' school next year.

Kenneth Norton: is a doctor. He thinks students need a good scientific education. As the school is near the town library, he doesn't support the new library plan.

I think Mrs Green will support ....

....

....

....

....

I think Colonel Brown will support ....

....

....

....

....

I think Patricia White will support ....

....

....

....

....

I think Kenneth Norton will support ....

....

....

....

....

7. Now, still in your groups, write a table showing what the school governors approve and disapprove of.

8. Using your table, complete the paragraphs in 6. (above).

Grammar Building   Conditionals (2)

Second conditional

1. John isn't happy about his school. He is complaining about it. Match each sentence on the left with a sentence on the right. Then rewrite the sentences using *if* + simple past tense + *would* or *could*. For example:

    QUESTION: My teacher shouts at me.   I don't work hard.
    ANSWER: *If* my teacher *didn't shout* at me, I *would* work hard.

The books are old.	I can't sit still.
The lessons are so long.	I get bad marks.
The desks are not comfortable.	I can't read them.
The school is far from home.	I have to take a bus.
The teacher doesn't like me.	I go to sleep.

2. George is about to leave school. He is full of dreams about the future and has made notes about what he might do. Change his notes into sentences using *if* + simple past tense + *would*. For example:

    QUESTION: Work hard ◗ pass exam.
    ANSWER: *If* I *worked* hard, I *would* pass my exam. If I passed my exam . . .

    Pass exam ◗ get job in bank ◗ earn a lot of money ◗ buy a yacht ◗ travel round the world ◗ have to take a long holiday ◗ lose my job ◗ be short of money ◗ sell the yacht ◗ buy a farm ◗ grow the best grapes in the country ◗ make a lot of money ◗ buy an aeroplane ◗

    Perhaps you can finish George's daydream for him.

Third conditional

3. The following ten sentences tell a story, but they are in the wrong order. Put them in the right order and rewrite them using *if* + past perfect tense + *would have*. For example:

    QUESTION: The bus was late, and I met the headmaster in the hall.
    ANSWER: *If* the bus *hadn't been late*, I *wouldn't have met* the headmaster in the hall.

    a The bus was late, and so I went to India.
    b I didn't phone my parents because they were at work.
    c No-one else was there, so he invited me into his study.
    d The headmaster saw me because the hall was empty.
    e His daughter was busy, so she couldn't go to India.

f My parents didn't stop me going because I already had the ticket.
g He had to ask someone quickly, because it was urgent.
h She couldn't use her ticket, so he gave it to me.
i I didn't disobey them because they didn't try to stop me.
j I didn't ask my parents then, so they didn't say no.

Mixed conditionals

4. Anna, Claire, Bill and David are discussing what they hope to study at college. Complete the conversation by putting the verbs in brackets into the correct form.

Claire: What are you going to study, Anna?
Anna: I don't know. My parents ¹(pay) for me only if I study law.
David: What would they do if you ²(not study) law?
Anna: They ³(not pay) for me, and I ⁴(not be able) to study. But I don't want to study law. If I had wanted to study law, I ⁵(not study) biology, would I?
Bill: I don't know what I should study. How should I choose?
Claire: It would depend on what you wanted to do afterwards. If you wanted to be a dentist, then you ⁶(choose) medicine.
David: What would I choose if I ⁷(want) to be a banker?
Anna: Do you want to be a banker?
David: My father says that if I study economics he ⁸(give) me a job in his business.
Anna: I thought you were going to be an artist! If you become a banker I ⁹(never speak) to you again!
David: But if I ¹⁰(become) a banker, I would have a lot of money and I ¹¹(be able) to retire early and become an artist.
Anna: If I ¹²(know) this before, I would never have agreed to go out with you.
Bill: If you had listened to me, you ¹³(not go out) with him in the first place!
Anna: And if I ¹⁴(want) your opinion, Bill Hill, I would have asked for it!

Extension   'If I had a thousand pounds . . .'

A great-uncle of yours has just died. In his will he has left you a thousand pounds – but it isn't for you! He wants you to give it to a person or an organization that needs it. The choice is entirely yours. Who would you give it to?

In pairs or small groups, decide who you would give the money to. Then tell your decision to the other groups. At the end, vote on which idea is best. You each have one vote.

Revision Transformations

Finish each of the following sentences in such a way that it means exactly the same as the sentence printed before it.

1. He didn't take his exam because he was ill.
    If ....

2. We never played sports at school because there wasn't a gym.
    If there ....

3. A language laboratory would help us to speak French much better.
    We ....

4. Our school hasn't got any computers because it can't afford them.
    Our school would ....

5. His chemistry marks were so bad that they wouldn't let him study medicine.
    If ....

6. We can't get jobs because we haven't got the right qualifications.
    If we ....

7. We didn't study chemistry because there wasn't a chemistry teacher.
    If there ....

8. If the exam hadn't been essential he wouldn't have taken it.
    Unless ....

9. Our school has an excellent science lab because the headmaster strongly believes in science.
    If the headmaster ....

10. I can't improve my French accent without spending some time in France.
    Unless I ....

Vocabulary Building   Word sets; word building

Word sets

1. Without looking back through the unit, write down all the words you can think of related to the topic 'Education'.
    Compare your list with the list you made at the beginning of the unit. How many new words have you learnt?

2. Find which words on your lists have opposites and write them down.
    Compare your list with a partner's or your dictionary.

3. Put the other words on your lists into 'word sets', like you did at the start of this unit on page 77. You might use sets like 'people', 'places', 'activities', etc.

   When you have done this, write the word sets from everyone in the class on the blackboard. Put them together wherever possible, i.e. 'rooms', 'places', and 'buildings' will obviously go together. Then write down all the words from the class in the suitable sets.

Word building

4. Use the word beginnings and word endings below to make as many words as possible.

BEGINNING	WORD	ENDING
over-	care	-able
un-	confident	-ful
under-	forget	-less
	prepared	
	success	
	teach	

   Is there anybody from your school-days that these words remind you of? Write the name of this person against the word and write why, or explain to a partner why, you have chosen this person.

Extension   'Set up your own school!'

In groups imagine that you are going to start a language school for teaching your own language to foreigners. Decide:
   – what part of town it should be in and why
   – how many rooms it should have
   – what furniture, equipment, etc. each room should contain
   – what kind of courses you should run
   – what other facilities you should have
   – what kind of teachers to employ
   – how much to charge for your courses

Then decide what name you will give your school, and how you will advertise it. You could design a brochure for your school and display it on your classroom wall.

UNIT EIGHT

BRITAIN

Foundations

1. Look at this map of Britain and label its three countries: Scotland, England and Wales.

2. Now look at the towns shown in the pictures on the map and label them correctly from the following: London, Stratford, Cambridge, Edinburgh.

3. In pairs or small groups, discuss what you know about Britain. What places do you know? What can you do if you go on holiday there? Can you add any places to the map?

4. Read the passage below quickly so that you can answer the following question. Do not try to fill in the blanks yet.

   What three aspects of Britain does the passage talk about?

   Many students visit Britain every summer either as tourists, or to learn the language, or to do a combination of the two. If you're thinking .... (1) visiting Britain, there are a .... (2) things that you should .... (3) ready for. Firstly, ... (4) weather can be very changeable – even in summer – so you .... (5) know what it's going to be like. It might be rainy or sunny, hot or cold, so you .... (6) be prepared for everything and .... (7) both summer clothes and warmer ones.
   Secondly, opening hours for shops, pubs, etc. can be very different from .... (8) countries. Shops normally open at 9.30 a.m. and .... (9) at 5.30 p.m. with no .... (10) in the middle of the day. .... (11) for pubs, their opening hours vary. Normal hours are 11.30 a.m. to 2.30 p.m. and 5.30 p.m. to 10.30 p.m., ... (12) you may find some pubs are open longer than this. You will also .... (13) discotheques open quite late, but generally speaking, night-life finishes early in Britain, and so .... (14) public transport.
   Finally, ... (15) word about eating. If you want to eat out there are lots of restaurants, but .... (16) tend to be expensive unless they are Indian or Chinese. Food in these is generally tasty and .... (17) value for money. But don't forget that you .... (18) eat in pubs and there the food is often good, varied and cheap, although if you're under eighteen they won't .... (19) you drink alcohol with your meal.
   One last thing: if you do come, ... (20) a great holiday!

5. Now choose the most suitable title for the passage:

   a Advice to tourists coming to Britain
   b Studying in Britain
   c Touring in Britain
   d Eating out in Britain

6. Read the passage again and complete the blanks.

7. List all the adjectives used in the passage to describe:

   a the weather
   b food

Extension

Advice to tourists in ....
To keep you healthy and safe.

We advise you to: We recommend you not to:

....

....

....

....

....

....

....

....

....

Fill in the above tables for your own town or country. For example, you might advise a tourist to use a mosquito net, and you might recommend a tourist not to eat shellfish.

When you have finished your table, compare and discuss what you have written with a partner.

Exam Training   Guided writing questions (2)

In Unit 7 you concentrated on practising skills to help you find the information you need in texts. In this unit you will practise using 'skimming' and 'scanning' skills to find information which is presented in different ways, e.g. in the form of maps, charts, diagrams, brochures, etc.

Information presented in charts, etc. can often look rather confusing. A lot of information is usually presented in a very small amount of space.

1.   Which of the following three approaches do you think is the best for finding information from charts and maps?

a   reading everything and making sure you understand it
b   skimming: looking quickly through the text to get an idea of what it means before you read it in more detail
c   scanning: deciding what you need to know from the text and searching through it only for that piece of information

2. Many charts, maps and diagrams use a lot of symbols, so when you have to find specific information from them it is very important that you read any headings and the key to the symbols very carefully – then you will not need to spend time looking at information that you do not need to answer the question.

Look at the information below. It is presented in different forms. Focus on the questions you need to answer, then scan the maps and graph to find the information you need.

a

1 Draw on a piece of paper all the weather symbols used in this chart.
2 What do all these symbols mean?
3 Which place would you like to be in tomorrow? Why?

b

1 Which of the three regions is generally the hottest in July?
2 Which of the three regions is generally the coldest in July?

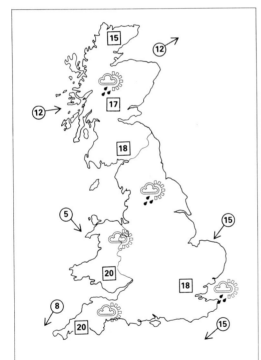

TOMORROW'S FORECAST

After a wet and cloudy start, most of the country will enjoy a dry day with some sunny periods. However, stronger winds in eastern districts of England will bring some light rain. Northern districts and Scotland should expect some rain, but with some periods of sunshine. In Wales and the south-west light winds and warm termperatures should bring fine weather for most of the day.

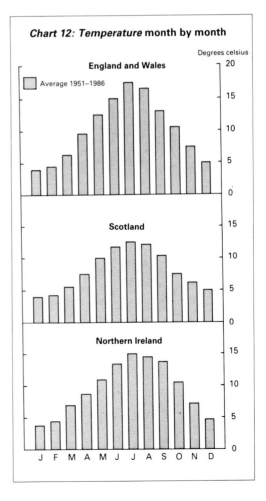

Chart 12: Temperature month by month

c

1 What does ⇌ mean?
2 What does ■ mean?
3 How far is London Zoo in Regent's Park from the Serpentine Cafeteria in Hyde Park?
4 What roads run around Green Park?
5 What is the tourist attraction in Hyde Park?
6 Make a list of at least five tourist attractions or places of interest within one mile of Buckingham Palace.

d Look at this list of some London hotels and also at the chart explaining the symbols it uses. Then write down five questions about anything on the chart or lists.

In groups, ask and answer one another's questions as quickly as possible.

CENTRAL LONDON

Hotel Diana
10–20 Leisham Gardens, W8

Recently modernised; near to museums, Albert Hall, antique shops and Hyde Park.
Bed & breakfast
£40–£50 double,
£25–£30 single.
Credit cards: Access, Visa, Diners, Amex.
❷ ❸ ❻ ❽ ❿

Aviemoor Hotel
32 Aviemore Rd., W14

Privately owned, friendly atmosphere. Colour TV, fridge & telephone in all rooms. 3 mins walk from Hyde Park.
Bed & breakfast
£45–£55 double
£30–£35 single.
❷ ❸ ❻ ❽ ❾

Hotel Colossus
22–28 Leisham Gardens, W8

Modernised Victorian building near shops, museums and parks. Airbus to Heathrow nearby.
Bed & breakfast
£45–£55 double,
£30–£35 single
Credit cards: Access, Visa, Diners, Amex.
❷ ❸ ❻ ❽ ❿

25 Holland Park Rd., W11
Family run boarding house with cooking facilities in all rooms. Minimum stay 1 month.
Bed & breakfast
£20–£25 double
❶ ❼ ❾

Holland Hotel
10 Ladgrove Avenue, W11

Quiet location; all bedrooms have colour TV and washbasin.
Bed & breakfast
£42–£52 double,
£28–£35 single
Credit cards: Access, Visa
❶ ❷ ❻ ❼ ❿

Mara Risha Hotel
30 Holland Park Rd., W11

Small, family run hotel with free parking. Close to Holland Park tube station.
Bed & breakfast
£35–£40 double,
£20–£25 single
❻ ❽

Key

❶ Telephone

❷ TV in all bedrooms

❸ Telephone in all bedrooms

❹ Garage or parking

❺ Outdoor sports area

❻ Children welcome

❼ Unlicensed (alcoholic drinks not served)

❽ Central heating throughout

❾ Room with shower

❿ Room with bath

3. During your holiday you meet some people in your hotel. They are all in London for different reasons. They want to go to the theatre and ask your opinion about which play they should go and see. Read the information below and answer the question.

    Which theatre would the following people probably like to go and see? Read the information and the theatre guide below, then complete the sentences saying which play each couple should go to and why.

    > Molly and George Turner live near London but they have not been to the theatre for years. They have decided to do something special for their 50th wedding anniversary. They both love music, but not classical music or opera.

    > Françoise Martin and her friend Beatrice Gautier are French university students who study English literature. They are on holiday in London and would like to go to a show which they would enjoy and which would also be useful for their studies.

    > Jill and Frank Marsden are on holiday in London from Australia. They are very much enjoying their holiday – meeting friends and going to pubs and restaurants and would like to go to something light-hearted, funny and entertaining.

    > Jack Barnes, Jane Hammond and Bill Sykes are all dance and drama students from a college in Scotland. They've come down to London for the weekend to see a very special show. They are especially interested in foreign touring companies.

DRURY LANE WC2 **42nd Street** Musical of the Year – Olivier Award 1984 Standard Drama Award 1984. London Theatre Critics Award 1984 Eves at 8.00. Sats at 5.00 & 8.30. Wed Mat at 3.00	**OPEN AIR THEATRE** NW1 SHAKESPEARE's **The Winter's Tale** July 25, 26 at 7.45 July 27 at 2.30 & 7.45 **A Midsummer Night's Dream** July 28, 29 at 7.45 July 30 at 2.30 & 7.45 in the open air!	**CAMBRIDGE** WC2 Two famous musical comedies presented by THE NEW D'OYLY CARTE OPERA COMPANY **Iolanthe** and **The Yeomen of the Guard** Eves at 7.30, Wed and Sat mats at 3.00 **SADLER'S WELLS** EC1 From August 16–September 3
DUKE OF YORKS WC2 ALAN AYCKBOURN's COMEDY **How The Other Half Loves** Directed by ALAN STRACHAN Mon–Fri at 8.00 Mats Thurs at 3.00. Sat at 5.00 & 8.15	**BARBICAN** EC2 Barbican Theatre ROYAL SHAKESPEARE COMPANY **The Merchant of Venice** July 25, 26 at 7.30 **Twelfth Night** July 27 at 7.30,	**Marcel Marceau** and members of his French mime Company Eves at 7.30, Sat Mats at 2.30 **ST. MARTIN'S** WC2 AGATHA CHRISTIE's Thriller . . . **The Mousetrap**
COVENT GARDEN WC2 Royal Opera House THE AUSTRALIAN BALLET **Sleeping Beauty** Tues, Wed, Fri, Sat at 7.30. Sat mat 2.30	July 28 at 2.00 & 7.30 **Julius Caesar** July 29 at 7.30, July 30 at 2.00 & 7.30	World's longest ever run! 36th Year SORRY No reduced prices at any time from any source Mon–Sat at 8.00, Mat Tues at 2.45, Sat at 5.00

Molly and George Turner should go and see ....

....

....

....

Françoise and Beatrice would enjoy ....

....

....

....

In my opinion the Marsdens ought to ....

....

....

....

I think that the students from Scotland should ....

....

....

....

Grammar Building   Statements and commands in indirect speech

1. You have a friend who is going to visit Britain. You want to give him or her advice in three different ways:

    a things they must do ....
    b things they should (not) do ....
    c general information ....

You are going to use the following verbs:

advise, inform, insist, recommend, suggest, tell, warn

Which verbs would you use for each kind of advice? Write the verbs in the spaces above. You may use some of the verbs more than once.

2. Now use the above verbs to make sentences, using the advice below. For example:

> *I will advise my friend to bring her umbrella.*
> or
> *I will recommend my friend to take some English lessons.*

a Bring both light and warm clothes for the summer.
b Don't forget to drive on the left.
c Why not stay in a bed and breakfast?
d Don't eat in restaurants unless you have a lot of money.
e Shops close on Wednesday afternoons.
f Visit Cambridge – it's beautiful!
g If I were you, I would stay outside London.
h You mustn't drink and drive.
i You have to leave pets in quarantine.
j Remember that Indian restaurants are generally cheap and good.
k Why not eat in pubs? They're very good and cheap.
l The pub opening hours vary from pub to pub.

3. 'My Mother Said . . .' Now imagine that you are in Britain. Some new friends keep inviting you to do things.
   Accept or refuse the invitations by telling your friends the advice your mother gave you. For example:

INVITATION: Let's go to the disco tonight.
REPLY: I can't. My mother said that I shouldn't dance with strange boys.

or

REPLY: What a good idea! My mother advised me to take lots of exercise.

a Let's go out for an Italian meal.
b Do you want to go to the cinema this evening?
c This party's boring! Let's go for a walk.
d Some friends are going to Brighton for the weekend. Will you come too?
e You can't miss this football match!
f It's a demonstration to Save the Whale. Everyone will be there.
g Haven't you been ice-skating before? You'll really enjoy it.
h Dangerous? No, hang-gliding is completely safe. Why not have a go?
i Come upstairs and listen to my jazz records.
j It's just a small house in the mountains, but it's very comfortable. Please come!

Extension   '. . . he said happily'

Below are some sentences that can be spoken in many different ways. In this game, the first student reads a sentence in a certain way, and then the second student reports how he said it, using the words '. . . he said happily' or '. . . he said angrily' or whatever. Then the third student, or anyone in the class, reports the whole sentence but without using the verb 'say'. For example:

Student 1:   (reads sadly) 'They drive on the left in England'
Student 2:   he said sadly:
Student 3:   He regretted that they drove on the left in England.

   You might find it useful to write a list of reporting verbs on the blackboard before starting, e.g. *state, promise, regret, complain, wish, agree, explain, insist, advise, warn*, etc.

1.   Big Ben is a bell, not a clock.
2.   The Channel Tunnel will take a long time to build.
3.   If you want to know the time, ask a policeman.
4.   Fish and chips can be very oily.
5.   It always rains on Sundays.
6.   There's just time for a nice cup of tea.
7.   Oh, take the dog for a walk!
8.   He likes to sing in the bath.
9.   It is not a boat, it's a bathtub.
10. I will never let you go.

Revision Transformations

Finish each of the following sentences in such a way that it means exactly the same as the sentence printed before it.

1.   'Paul, why don't you go by ferry?' Jane said.
     Jane suggested ....

2.   'Don't go out late by yourself,' my friend told me.
     My friend advised me ....

3.   When I saw the rain I remembered to take my umbrella.
     The rain reminded ....

4.   'Don't park your car on double yellow lines' the notice said.
     The notice warned people ....

5.   'I haven't got any money left,' Paul said to me.
     Paul told ....

6.   'Edinburgh is the capital of Scotland,' the teacher told the class.
     The teacher informed ....

7. 'I'm afraid you can't take guns into Britain,' the customs officer told the passenger.
The customs officer refused ....

8. 'This bank closes at three p.m.' said the notice.
Customers were notified ....

9. 'You must go to a pub when you go to England,' the teacher told her students.
The teacher recommended ....

10. 'It can rain a lot in Britain in the summer,' the girl told her friend.
The girl ....

Vocabulary Building   Preposition phrases

In English you often find fixed expressions (words which are found together in common everyday speech) made up of a preposition plus a noun or an adverb. For example *on*, *at*, *in*, *by* + a noun or adverb, such as *on time*, *at once*, *in the end*, *by heart*. The vocabulary questions in the *Use of English* paper sometimes test your knowledge of expressions of this type.

1. Look at the chart below of expressions with *at* and match them to their meanings by writing the prepositions plus the correct word into the blanks. The first one has been done for you.

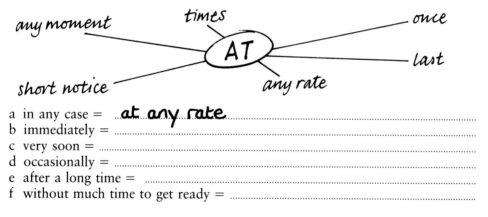

a in any case = *at any rate* ....
b immediately = ...
c very soon = ...
d occasionally = ...
e after a long time = ...
f without much time to get ready = ...

2. Read the following passage and fill in each blank with one of the expressions above.

   In the eighties unemployment has been a major problem in the UK. Jack, for example, was unemployed for years. Every day while his wife was out at work he sat reading the newspaper, looking for a job. (a) .... he got very depressed. There was never anything suitable for a man in his forties – (b) ...., that's how it seemed. One day though things changed. His former boss phoned him and asked him if he could come back to work the next day. He said he realized that he was asking him (c) ....

'Don't worry – I can start (d) ....,' Jack replied. 'I will be in the office tomorrow morning at 9.00 on the dot.' (e) .... he had found a job!

3. Now get into groups and choose one of the boxes below. Use your dictionary to check any of the expressions you don't understand. Write sentences, or a story as above, which contain each of the phrases in your box. Check with your teacher that the sentences are correct.
    Leave a blank for each phrase. Give your sentences or story to another group and see if they can fill in your blanks with the correct phrase.

BY	IN	OUT OF	preposition + TIME
chance	common	breath	at a time
far	the end	danger	at times
heart	a hurry	date	at the same time
mistake	love	doors	in time
yourself	other words	sight	on time
	time	work	

Word Building

4. Not all words make verbs, adjectives, etc. by adding word endings and beginnings. Look at the nouns below and write the adjectives that come from them in the blanks. Which nouns formed an adjective by adding something? Which did not?

strength ....   patience ....
confidence ....   pride ....
courage ....   wisdom ....
health ....

Now write the opposites of the words you have just written above.

Extension　　　Your country through facts and figures

Collect together some charts, graphs, maps, brochures, adverts, etc. about any aspect of your country, e.g. tourism or food, and put them onto a big piece of paper to make a poster. Add any writing to the poster that makes the pictures clearer. The aim is to present information about your country as clearly as possible.
    When the whole group has prepared their posters, display them on a wall in the classroom or in your school. If possible, ask another group of students to come and look at your posters. Try to persuade as many people as you can to come and visit your country!

UNIT NINE

THE MEDIA

Foundations

1. Look at the 'spider' diagram below of the media. In ten minutes add as many words as you can think of related to each type of medium. The diagram has been started for you.

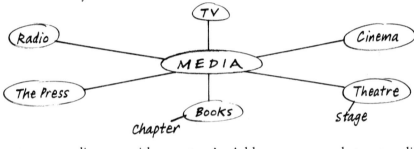

2. Compare your diagram with a partner's. Add any new words to your diagram.

3. Look at the pictures below and describe what you can see in them. What part of the above diagram do you think they relate to?

4. Read the passage below quickly so that you can answer the following
    questions. Do not try to fill in the blanks yet.

    a What is 'Children's Express'?
    b How do the pictures above relate to the passage?

    Children's Express is a unique organization that started twelve years ago
    with the slogan 'BY CHILDREN FOR EVERYBODY'. The idea behind
    the articles, which are .... (1) in over thirty papers across
    .... (2) USA as .... (3) as in New Zealand and
    Australia, is to encourage readers .... (4) look at important issues
    from the .... (5) of view of children and young people.
       In their New York office the 200 young reporters can choose
    .... (6) story they want to work on, depending .... (7)
    what they are .... (8) in. On any story, a team of three or four,
    usually under thirteen and sometimes as young .... (9) eight,
    work with an assistant editor. Interviews .... (10) done using
    tape-recorders and are then typed out by adult workers. The ....
    (11) interesting articles are then selected .... (12) a teenage
    assistant editor and an adult Children's Express editor.
       Children's Express teams have interviewed local politicians and
    presidential candidates. They have covered stories on Chernobyl and
    Kampuchea and have investigated difficult social problems .... (13)
    as violence .... (14) the family. They also .... (15)
    articles in Spanish for the large .... (16) of Spanish American
    readers. Recently they have announced that they're .... (17) to
    produce a weekly TV news programme, starting .... (18) year.
    Ten-year-old Laurel is to .... (19) one of the presenters of the
    programme because she is not embarrassed about asking important people
    difficult questions. To Laurel, working on a TV .... (20) is just
    'fun'!

5. This passage, together with the picture above, came from a newspaper report.
    In pairs or small groups, decide on what headline you think it should have.

6. Read the passage again and complete the blanks.

7. Underline all the words in the passage related to the media.

Extension   'Read all about it!'

Why don't you start your own newspaper or newsboard at your school? If that
seems a bit over-ambitious, then try to produce a newsletter for other students in
your school.

In class discuss:
- how useful and/or popular a newsletter, etc. might be
- what kind of publications it would be most practical to produce
- how you would find your news
- who would do what jobs
- who you would want to interview
- what other things you might include
- how you could publicize your news
- any other points you can think of

If you all agree that the idea is a good one and worth doing, you could perhaps write to other students in your school and to teachers telling them about it. Or you could do a sample and display it on the wall of your classroom. Get comments on how it could be improved.

Exam Training   Guided writing questions (3)

In Units 7 and 8 you practised skills to help you pick out relevant information from texts and make notes from that information.

In this unit you will practise skills to help you write good paragraphs in correct English.

1. Look at the following example of a text from a guided writing question, so that you can fill in the table at the end. The paragraphs that you normally have to complete have been taken out.

    Read the following passages about a proposed music festival in the small town of Pepperton.

From Guide to Pepperton

PEPPERTON: Pop. 30,000 Small town in the heart of the English countryside; famous for its beautiful parks near the River Severn. Very popular holiday resort for elderly people. Very old and beautiful town centre.

SUMMER ROCK FESTIVAL
New bands!
Great music!
Come and dance
the day away!
DATE: July 6th–20th
PLACE: River Park
TIME: 2.00pm until late

Some letters from the Pepperton Echo

Dear Sir

It is scandalous that the council is allowing a rock music festival to take place. It must be cancelled. Many people enjoy sitting peacefully in River Park and they will not be able to do so with the noise of that awful music polluting the air. Tourism is very important for the prosperity of our town, and many of our tourists, who are older people, will be most upset by this festival. Young people nowadays are so thoughtless!

I should warn you that the Residents' Association is considering taking some action.

Yours sincerely

Gordon Smith
Chairman, Pepperton Residents Association.

Dear Sir

A lot of people are complaining about the music festival which will take place in July.

As organizer of the festival, I think that everyone in the town should support it. Young people in Pepperton have nowhere to go and nothing to do at night. There are always violent fights in the centre of town at weekends – every week you write reports about them in your paper.

The festival will give our young people a chance to express themselves and their feelings and to feel that at last the town is doing something for them.

Mick Tagger
Organizer of the Summer Rock Festival

Dear Sir

I am writing to you about the summer festival. As a mother of two teenage children who are always complaining about how bored they are, I think it is a wonderful idea. I can understand, however, why the older people in the town are upset. Why doesn't the council ask the organizers to make it a festival for the whole community? They could have classical music as well as rock – and they could involve everyone.

Yours sincerely

Joan Bennett

PEPPERTON TOWN COUNCIL
To: Public Entertainments Officer
From: Leader of the Council

I am becomng worried about the summer festival. A lot of people have written to me complaining about it. Do you think we should cancel it – especially because there will be an election in August?

A lot of the older residents in the town seem very annoyed. I have had a very angry letter from Gordon Smith – and you know how powerful he is!

Please let me know what you think as soon as possible.

Read the texts and complete the following table in note form.

NAME	REASONS FOR FESTIVAL	REASONS AGAINST FESTIVAL

2. In all guided writing questions you first need to pick out all the relevant information from the texts. You then have to write short paragraphs giving your decisions or choices and your reasons for making them. To do this, you need to be able to write grammatically accurate sentences. You will particularly need to use linking words and phrases that:

a list a number of ideas
b introduce reasons
c add more reasons to support points already made
d introduce points which are the opposite of what has been said before
e sum up your points and conclude

   Match the five groups of linking words and phrases below with the five groups above.

A In other words   B Firstly/First of all
   To conclude   Secondly/Next
   In conclusion   Thirdly
   To sum up   The first point is
                                 The final point
                                 Lastly/Finally

C Besides   D Because/since/as
   What's more   So
   Not only . . . but also . . . Therefore
                                 As a result

E But
   However
   In spite of
   Although
   On the other hand

3. A student has written the following notes on the first letter about the summer rock festival.

NAME	REASONS FOR FESTIVAL	REASONS AGAINST FESTIVAL
Gordon Smith		noise- stop tourists - upset old people

   Complete the paragraph she has written using her notes with the words in the box below.

(a) .... Gordon Smith proposes that the summer rock festival should be stopped (b) .... he thinks that tourists will be frightened away from the town. (c) .... he is frightened that the old people will not be able to sit in peace in the park near the river.

> BECAUSE   FIRSTLY   WHAT'S MORE

4. Look at your notes for the other comments about the festival, and write a paragraph for each one. Blank out the linking words and phrases that you have used and exchange your paragraphs with another student. Can you complete each other's blanks?

5. To write good correct paragraphs you do not only need to be able to use linking words and phrases accurately. You also need to use expressions for giving your opinion and for justifying your choice. Look at the two boxes of useful expressions below.

> In my opinion/view
> I believe/feel that
> As I see it
> It seems to me that

> One of the advantages/disadvantages of ... is ...
> The main advantage/disadvantage of ... is ...
> The main drawback/problem with ... is ...

   Now imagine that you are a newspaper reporter and you have to write about the festival. Try to summarize all the views about the festival using the expressions and link words above to help you.

Extension   'What's on?'

In groups of three or four find out what kind of entertainment is available for young people in the area where you live. Make a list of some of the films and theatre shows, etc. that are currently on.

Write a short description of some you know about, saying what kind of film or show etc. they are, what they are about, how good they are and why. Display your descriptions on the classroom wall.

Choose one film or show that you have not seen and which you would like to go to. Invite or persuade at least two other people to come with you – giving good reasons why they should come!

Grammar Building   Questions in reported speech

1. You are the editor of your local newspaper. You have just heard that the Minister of Education is visiting your area to make a big speech. You think he is going to announce changes to the education system which might include:
    * new training schemes for young people
    * putting up the school-leaving age
    * a new exam for school leavers
    * abolishing private education
    You have heard rumours that the Minister has an unhappy home life, and also that he has just had a big argument with the Prime Minister.

    You are sending your best reporter to interview him, but first you want to give your reporter advice about what to ask.

    In pairs or groups, decide what questions you should ask the Minister, and then make sentences to tell your reporter what to ask. Begin each sentence with the words 'You must ask him . . .'

    Remember that the Minister may not want to answer some questions; you will have to ask your questions carefully!

2. Report the following questions using the words in brackets to help you. For example:

    QUESTION?   Did you hear a loud bang? (The policeman)
    ANSWER: *The policeman asked if I had heard a loud bang.*

    a Now, where did I put my keys?   (The old man)
    b Is there a garage near here?   (A stranger)
    c When are we filming the snow scene?   (The film director)
    d Will this plan really create new jobs?   (The reporter)
    e Would you like to come to dinner tonight? (Mary)
    f Haven't we met before?   (The actress)
    g May I help you with your suitcase?   (The young man)
    h Why don't we go to the cinema instead?   (John's mother)
    i Are you sure the theatre is in Green Street? (The taxi driver)
    j Why does ice float?   (The teacher)

3. You can report questions without using the verb *ask*. Complete the following reported questions so that they mean the same as the questions in 2 above.

    a The old man wondered . . .
    b A stranger enquired . . .
    c The film director wanted to know . . .
    d The reporter doubted . . .
    e Mary invited . . .
    f The actress couldn't remember . . .
    g The young man offered . . .
    h John's mother suggested . . .
    i The taxi driver questioned . . .
    j The teacher wanted us to tell her . . .

Extension   'Why did they ask you that?'

In this game you must pretend that you have just been to a job interview. You must not tell the other students what job the interview was for, and you must not use the name of the job, but you may report the questions that you were asked at the interview.

    Of course, you have to report questions that will help the other students guess the correct job. The other students have to guess what the job is as quickly as possible. For example:

You:	They asked me if I was frightened of animals.
Them:	Do you want to be a vet?
You:	No. They asked me if I liked children.
Them:	Do you want to work in a zoo?
You:	No. They asked me if I wanted to travel.
Them:	Do you want to work in a circus?
You:	Yes.

Vocabulary Building   Compound words

In English nouns, adjectives and adverbs often combine with other words to form new words. These are compound words and they can be written as two words (e.g. *post office*), as one word with a hyphen (e.g. *blue-eyed*, *newly-wed*) or as a single word (e.g. *waterproof*).

    The vocabulary questions in the *Use of English* paper often test your knowledge of compound words, for example:

    The article was written by a well-................. journalist.

    There are many different compound words in English and a learner's dictionary can help you to find and remember them. Look at this dictionary entry for **news**: it shows you that **newsagent**, etc. are all compound words that can be made with **news**.

news /njuːz/ *nu* (also *attrib*) new or fresh information; reports(s) of what has most recently happened: *Have you heard the news about the air disaster? The news is bad. Here are the news headlines. Here are some interesting pieces/bits of news. That's news to me* (= I did not know that). *That's no news to me* (= I already know that). **no news is good news** while there is no information we, you etc can still hope.
   'news·agent *nc* a person, business that sells newspapers, magazines etc.
   'news·flash *nc* short piece of important news on television or radio.
   'news-letter *nc* a letter or printed paper sent out to members of a society etc.
   'news·paper *nc* a printed publication, usually issued daily, with news, advertisements etc.
   'news-reader *nc* **(a)** a person who regularly reads a particular newspaper. **(b)** a person who reads the news aloud on the radio or TV.
   'news-stand *nc* a stall in the street for the sale of newspapers etc.
   'news·worthy *adj* sufficiently interesting for reporting, e.g. in a newspaper.

   To help you remember compound words, it might be useful to keep a list of them, adding new ones to the list every time you come across one.

1.   Make compound words related to the topic 'The media' by putting the words below into the correct group, e.g. *bookcase, film show*. NOTE: Some of the words may go into more than one group.

BOOK	FILM	RADIO	TELEVISION

director   case   satellite   festival
programme   station   seller   producer
show   set   announcer   aerial
shop   stall   broadcast   star
advertisement

Use your dictionary to check the spelling once you have completed the table.

2.   How many more examples of compound words can you find in this unit?

Word building

3. Use the word endings below to make as many words as possible within three
    minutes.

WORD	ENDING
announce	-er
advert	-ing
edit	-ism
journal	-ist
publish	-ize
report	-ment
	-or

Who has the most words? Compare your list with a partner's or your
dictionary.

Extension   'Producers . . . Directors!'

What do you think of television programmes? Is there a good mixture of
programmes available or are there too many of certain kinds? What kind of
programmes would you like to see more of?

In groups, work out a schedule for your ideal evening's television entertainment.
You may have to work very hard to persuade members of the group that they
want to see the same kind of programmes as you.

Compare your schedule with that of other groups. Whose looks the most
interesting?

PRACTICE PAPER ONE

> *This Practice Paper is modelled closely on authentic examinations. Try to complete it under authentic examination conditions, keeping to the time limit, and without the help of a dictionary.*

USE OF ENGLISH   2 hours

1. *Fill each of the numbered blanks in the following passage. Use only* **one** *word in each space.*

Forty years ago, people from the north of Europe began to invade the Mediterranean. For hundreds of years, the population of Europe had been .... (1) at an enormous rate. In the fifteenth century it stood at approximately fifty million. By the end of the eighteenth century .... (2) had doubled, and by the end of the nineteenth century it was more .... (3) four hundred million.

   The majority of this expanding population did .... (4) earn their living in the old way, directly from the land or sea, ... (5) in the new industrialized cities of northern Europe.

   In .... (6) first years of the twentieth century, most of .... (7) remained there. Transport was slow, difficult and expensive and .... (8) the wealthy could afford .... (9) leave the wetter, cloudier parts of Europe and .... (10) down to the sunny shores of the Mediterranean. A few towns along the coast of Italy and southern France began to .... (11) expensive hotels .... (12) visitors could stay, but their numbers were still relatively .... (13).

   Then, after the Second World War, the introduction of cheap air travel, together .... (14) greater prosperity for everybody, ... (15) a visit to the Mediterranean possible for the majority of Europeans. And .... (16) were now some 490 million of them.

   The result .... (17) a huge annual migration. .... (18) the summer of 1973, when a detailed survey was carried .... (19), sixty million people travelled south to the sea. Now, the annual total is thought to be more than a hundred million. Most of them come during the short, three month summer season, and stay .... (20) a few hundred yards of the coast.

2. *Finish each of the following sentences in such a way that it means exactly the same as the sentence printed before it.*

   EXAMPLE: Despite the rain, they decided to go for a walk.
   ANSWER: Although *it was raining, they decided to go for a walk.*

   a) George and Alan haven't finished university yet.
      George and Alan are ....

   b) Nobody heard Sheila's cry for help.
      Sheila's ....

   c) Many teachers would rather go on holiday in the summer than work for extra money.
      Many teachers prefer ....

   d) Wouldn't it be marvellous to live in a house like that!
      I wish ....

   e) We enjoyed ourselves in the mountains despite the bad weather.
      Although ....

   f) I applied for the job because my father encouraged me.
      If my father ....

   g) Elizabeth's children didn't go to school yesterday because they had flu.
      Elizabeth's children were prevented ....

   h) 'Is it still raining?' Susan asked.
      Susan wanted to know ....

   i) The house was much bigger than Jill had thought.
      Jill hadn't realized ....

   j) John said he wouldn't pay the bill.
      John refused ....

3. *The word in capitals at the end of the following sentences can be used to form a word that fits suitably in the blank space. Fill each blank in this way.*

   EXAMPLES: She said 'Thank you' in a most *friendly* way.   FRIEND
   My teacher *encouraged* me to take the exam.   COURAGE

   a) Miriam's .... was the happiest time of her life.   CHILD

   b) Because her skirt was too short, Marta decided to .... it.   LONG

   c) Uncle Jack picked up a .... of sweets and gave them to the children.   HAND

   d) I sent the steak back because it was .... It was burnt black!   COOK

   e) After the meeting, the managing director decided to hand in his
      ....   RESIGN

4. *Complete the following sentences by writing in the space provided a suitable word meaning the opposite of the word in capital letters.*

   EXAMPLE: His sister was very TALL but his younger brother was very *short*.

   a) As prices in the famous holiday resort INCREASED the number of tourists ....

   b) Some people think that laziness is a STRENGTH, not a ....

   c) At school our history lessons are really INTERESTING but our geography lessons are awfully ....

   d) He had a reputation for being rather MEAN but in fact he was a very .... man.

   e) Fiona used to SPEND a lot of money every month but now she is .... to buy a flat.

5. *Make all the changes and additions necessary to produce, from the following set of words and phrases, sentences which together make a complete letter. Note carefully from the example what kind of alterations need to be made. Write each sentence in the space provided.*

   EXAMPLES: I write/you/thank you very much/your letter.
   ANSWER: *I am writing to you to thank you very much for your letter.*

   Dear Sir or Madam.

   I write/enquire/courses you run/your school/summer.

   a) ....

   First/all, I be grateful/you tell me/cost of the courses.

   b) ....

   Then, I also like/know/kind/accommodation you provide.

   c) ....

   Be/school residential or do you find us rooms/English families?

   d) ....

   If/have/brochure I wonder/you send me one?

   e) ....

   I already study English/five years.

   f) ....

   I be particularly interested/intensive courses/business English.

   g) ....

   I look forward/hear/you and thank/in advance/your co-operation.

   h) ....

   Yours faithfully,

6. Below are extracts from a guide to restaurants in London. There is also a description of four groups of people who want to go out to dinner in London tonight.

Decide which restaurant each group of people will probably go to. Write your answers, giving reasons for your choices in the spaces provided on page 115.

Greens Vegetarian Restaurant
17, Flint Street.
Cheap, lively; good Jazz singer.
Open 7 p.m. to midnight.

Fredericks
1, Holme Road.
Fish only – excellent;
expensive, quiet.
Open 7.30–10.30 p.m.

Chez Catherine
13, Mandale Street.
The best French food in
town, romantic atmosphere;
expensive, credit cards accepted.
Open 7–11 p.m.

Da Gino
19, Wallbury Street.
Italian food, usually
well-cooked. Live Italian
music, friendly atmosphere;
quite cheap.
Open 8–11.30 p.m.

Kyoto Japanese Restaurant
16, Flight Street.
Excellent – if you like
Japanese food; quiet.
Open 7–11.30 p.m.

The English Rose
31, Regent Row.
Very good traditional English
food, beautifully decorated
restaurant; excellent service.
Open 7–10 p.m.

Jenny Matthews	once worked in Japan and China. She loves all oriental food. She doesn't have much money and would like to take her Japanese friend, who is visiting London, to somewhere unusual.
Michael Barnet	is a company director and wants to invite his new girlfriend, an opera-singer, out to dinner. He would like to go somewhere quiet.

Ana and Pedro Gomez   are a Spanish couple who are visiting London from Madrid. They love eating good food and eating late. They enjoy the excitement and noise of busy, popular restaurants. Ana is vegetarian, but Pedro dislikes vegetarian food.

Jill Edwards   and her five friends from the office would like an interesting meal in quiet surroundings so that they can plan their summer holidays together. They can't go to dinner before 9.30 p.m.

In my opinion Jenny Matthews..

....

....

....

....

I think that Michael Barnet...

....

....

....

....

As for Ana and Pedro Gomez..

....

....

....

....

Finally, Jill Edwards ....

....

....

....

....

PRACTICE PAPER TWO

> *This Practice Paper is modelled closely on authentic examinations. Try to complete it under authentic examination conditions, keeping to the time limit, and without the help of a dictionary.*

USE OF ENGLISH   2 hours

1. *Fill each of the numbered blanks in the following passage. Use only **one** word in each space.*

    The position of women in Britain has changed considerably this century, particularly within the last twenty years, and the main change has been towards greater equality .... (1) men.
       Up .... (2) the early part of this century a woman's .... (3) role was that of wife and mother. Even in families where women .... (4) out to work they still had to run the home and look .... (5) the children. During the two World Wars women took over many jobs which .... (6) had only been done by men. Afterwards, women continued .... (7) work alongside men .... (8) often in lower-status, less well-paid .... (9).
       Gradually it became accepted that women wanted to have their .... (10) careers and .... (11) the same pay as men for the .... (12) job. Laws were passed to protect them .... (13) discrimination.
       Today, ... (14) are able to lead lives of greater variety. Many choose .... (15) to work and to concentrate on .... (16) families instead. However, many .... (17) to work and accept help in caring .... (18) their children from various private or state facilities .... (19) as child-minders and nursery schools. Fathers are also more involved in child care than they used to be, in some cases .... (20) at home while the mother goes out to work.

2. *Finish each of the following sentences in such a way that it means exactly the same as the sentence printed before it.*

    EXAMPLE: Despite the rain, they decided to go for a walk.
    ANSWER: Although *it was raining, they decided to go for a walk.*

a) John last saw his parents ten years ago.
John hasn't ....

b) I really must go to the dentist.
It's time ....

c) It wasn't until 3 a.m. that they went to bed.
They only ....

d) It's too cold to go outside without a coat.
It isn't...

e) 'If I were you, Tom, I'd look for a new job,' said Bill.
Bill advised ....

f) Ann wished she hadn't spent so much money.
Ann regretted ....

g) As well as speaking Chinese, Janet also speaks Arabic.
Not only...

h) Jane said she'd never seen such a lovely beach before.
'This is the ....

i) It is forbidden to smoke in cinemas.
You ....

j) You can eat this food directly from the packet.
This food ....

3. *Complete each of the following sentences with an expression formed from* **bring**. *Write in one word for each blank space.*

EXAMPLE: In spite of all his difficulties James brought *off* the deal.

a) The government wants to bring .... new laws about drinking and driving next year.

b) Remember, Sonya, you must bring these books .... to the library when you have finished reading them.

c) When I was young, children were brought .... very strictly by their parents.

d) When John fainted, his wife brought him .... with a glass of brandy.

e) The teacher decided to bring .... the question of exam organization at the next staff meeting.

4. *Complete the following sentences with* **one** *appropriate word connected with the subject of* **houses**.

    EXAMPLE: Mary has a nice sunny room on the top *floor*.

    a) Mauro realized there must be a hole in the .... when the rain started dripping through the ceiling.

    b) Don't leave your car outside. Put it in the ....

    c) Rather than buying a flat, many people prefer to .... one.

    d) It's a nice flat with a lovely .... so we can sit outside when the weather is fine.

    e) We were miserably cold when we moved into our new house last winter because the central .... wasn't working.

5. *Jill and Susan are comparing their summer holidays. Fill in the parts of the dialogue, numbered (1) to (6), which have been left blank.*

    Jill: Hi, Susan! (1) ....?
    Susan: Oh, it was absolutely fantastic. Never had such a great time. How about yours?
    Jill: It was awful. Absolutely awful.
    Susan: Oh no, (2) ....?
    Jill: Everything – bad food, bad weather, bad hotel, horrible beach – everything.
    Susan: Oh, I'm so sorry. (3) ....?
    Jill: No, it was the first time. We saw it in one of those travel brochures. Anyway we won't go there again.
    Susan: Right. Where (4) .... next year? You could come with me if you like. We had such a fantastic time that we've already decided to go back to the same place.
    Jill: (5) ....?
    Susan: A tiny village with lots of sand, sun, good restaurants, and hardly any other tourists.
    Jill: Did (6) ....?
    Susan: No, some friends told us about it. They'd been there the year before. Why don't you come with us?
    Jill: Well, it's certainly worth thinking about. Thanks very much.

6. *Below you will find a newspaper report, some notes taken by telephone, and an extract from a guidebook. They all contain details about summer courses at four English language teaching colleges. There are also details about three people who want to choose a summer course. Using this information, complete the paragraphs on page 119, saying which course each person will probably choose, and giving reasons for your choice.*

BUCKLEY MANOR: 5 mins from town centre; large grounds – good for sports (tennis, soccer, etc.); ages 7–18; cheap.

TRAINING FOR ENGLISH?

What's the quickest way to learn English? By train, of course! The new Moving School is taking 100 students, aged between 15 and 20, on a tour of Britain by train. The students will sleep and eat on the train, and they will have English language classes while they are travelling to the next town. They expect to visit 15 towns in different parts of Britain.

A strange way to learn English, you might think. But a good way to see England – if you have a lot of money to spare!

	Location	Fees	Class size	Ages	Sports etc.	Special interest
Locksley Hall	Bex-on-Sea	High	Large	All	Sailing; swimming	Literature classes
Learning Centre	London	High	Small	All	None	Business English

Arlette Menle: 38 years old; managing director of cheese factory in Holland; very keen sailor; needs intensive English course for her work.

Yannis Spiridis: 17 years old; railway enthusiast; doesn't have much money; needs English revision for exam at his school in Greece.

Marguerite Lanson: 56 years old; French; wants to see England; likes reading very much; likes eating fish.

I think Arlette will choose ....

....

....

....

....

....

Yannis will probably choose ....

....

....

....

....

....

The best choice for Marguerite is ....

....

....

....

....

....

KEY

STARTER UNIT

Quiz

1. 2 hours.
2. grammar, vocabulary, ability to work to time limits, reading, writing.

Sample Paper

1. (1) two/so (2) corner (3) turned/froze (4) but (5) in/through
   (6) next/following (7) through (8) This/It (9) coming/moving/
   reaching (10) began/started (11) only/just (12) very (13) by/under
   (14) felt (15) then/next/suddenly (16) from/off (17) If (18) anything
   (19) anyone/anybody/you (20) it

2. a ... hot/warm enough to go swimming today.
   b ... staying/to stay at home than going/to go to a bad film.
   ... staying at home to going to a bad film.
   c ... a beautiful day!' exclaimed George.
   d ... of feeling ill/of the fact that he felt ill, Jeremy still went to work.
   e ... was such an awful meal that they refused to pay the bill.
   f ... finished your homework yet?
   g ... Anne to stay to/for dinner.
   h ... will be stolen unless you lock it.
   i ... (that) I've been to a safari park.
   j ... taking the money/that he had taken the money.

3. a landed b lengthen c bright d lazy e fresh.

4. a height b weakness c irrelevant d relationship e likeable
   f uncomfortable g daily h careless.

5. a I'm/I am writing to ask you if you'd/you would like to come on holiday
     with us.
   b We had such a nice time together in Scotland last year.
   c So I think/thought/was thinking it'd/it would be nice to go somewhere
     together again this year.

d We are/were thinking of visiting the islands off the coast of Yugoslavia in August.

e We're going/are going to go by car from London to Venice, (from) where we'll/we will get the ferry to Porec.

f Then we'll/we will camp when we get to the islands.

g We're/are really looking forward to going there.

h We hope very much you'll be able to join us.

i Please let us know so we can make arrangements.

6. Possible answers:
Some people believe the Manfredia nuclear plant should be closed because they think it causes cancer, especially in children. They also believe it is a source of pollution which has spoilt the fishing trade and ruined farming lands.

Some people believe the Manfredia nuclear plant should be kept open because it employs lots of people in an area of high unemployment and also provides cheap energy. What's more they say there's no reason to close the plant because it threatens health as there's no proof that the plant is responsible for the increase in cancer deaths.

I think the best thing to do is to carry out more research into the link between nuclear plants and death from cancer. This needs to be carried out urgently and very carefully.

UNIT ONE

Foundations

4. a Bill and Cathy
    b Tom
    c They used to, but Tom has left home now and Bill lives a few streets away.

5. c

Exam Training

3. (3) c   (4) c   (5) c   (6) a   (7) b   (8) b   (9) c
    (10) a

4. Helpful words:
    (6) used, do   (9) no wish, live, from home
    (7) Then, was Cathy   (10) let, her, whatever she liked
    (8) Cathy, worked

5. (11) to   (12) when   (13) like/know   (14) anything
    (15) himself   (16) got/became   (17) for   (18) stopped
    (19) one   (20) left

Grammar Building

2. a He thought he was wonderful/he was 'a kind of God'.
    b He must have gone to prison.
    c He may have been the child's uncle/a lodger at the child's house/a criminal
       in hiding.

Revision Transformations

  2. '. . .not visit Jane/her/my daughter,' Jane's father told me.
  3. . . . be pleased about your daughter's new job.
  4. . . . sometimes be difficult to look after young children.
  5. . . . have to start school at the age of five.
  6. . . . Mary could go to the disco.
  7. . . . had to look after his elderly parents.
  8. . . . must tell him the truth.
  9. . . . may/might get divorced.
 10. . . . need to have larger families.

Vocabulary Building

1. generous – selfish,   cynical – romantic,   happy – miserable,
    insecure – confident,   relaxed – tense,   aggressive – defensive,
    optimistic – pessimistic,   tough – soft,   rude – polite

UNIT TWO

Foundations

1. Yacht, hot-air balloon, hovercraft, barge, cable-car, parachute.

4. a Today's overcrowded transport systems.
    b It changes to talk about transport in the future.

5. b

6. (1) such   (2) from   (3) has   (4) with/by   (5) each   (6) have/cause   (7) so
    (8) can   (9) many   (10) enough/sufficient   (11) though/however   (12) In
    (13) be   (14) in/from   (15) which   (16) directed/driven/controlled   (17) to
    (18) be/become   (19) as/since/because   (20) it/that

7. air pollution, ill-health, blocked roads, bad and aggressive driving, crowded
    buses and trains.

8. a traffic jam   b accidents   c crowded   d replaced   e vehicles   f lead
    g car park   h traffic   i banned

Exam Training

2. It was such a hot plate (that) James couldn't pick it up.

3. by them

4. Change *remember* to *forget*: She didn't forget to give you the key, did she?

5. Sally wishes people wouldn't call her Mrs Jones.
    Charles regretted not buying/having bought the old boat.

6. . . .where the front door was/is.

7. a . . . usually as/so quick to travel by road as by train.
    b . . . hadn't been a strike Bill would have gone to work.
    c . . . fly than go by boat.
    d . . . expensive for us to fly to Madrid.
    e . . . was so difficult that it took John nearly ten hours.
    f . . . don't always need to/have to show your passport at the border.
    g . . . a new bridge is built, the traffic problems will get worse.
    h . . . building the new motorway to the coast.
    i . . . our going to the island by hydrofoil.
    j . . . told the passengers not to forget to take all their hand luggage with
       them.

Grammar Building

1. g, c, b, e, h, d, i, f, j, a

Sentence	Simple past	Past continuous	Present perfect	used to
a	travelled was		have become	
b	was cleaned			
c	got bought			

Sentence	Simple past	Past continuous	Present perfect	used to
d	broke		has never recovered	
e	had	was riding		
f	came across	was searching		
g				used to travel
h	happened		have never been able	
i	decided			
j	fell bought		have had	

You can only change the verb forms in b and g without changing the meaning. You can use the past tense instead of 'used to' or vice-versa, because it is possible to use the past tense for habitual past actions.

2. b have never been c have driven d went e operated f bought
g never travelled/used to travel h have had i never dreamt j had
k have not bought l have already built m Have you ever visited . . .?

Revision Transformations

1. . . . travelled by tram since I was a child.
2. . . . flown/been flying planes for ten years.
3. . . . have already been banned from the centre of some cities.
4. . . . did they first use battery-powered cars?
5. . . . as cheap as it was/used to be.
6. . . . the first time I've been on a transatlantic flight.
7. . . . cycle as much as she used to.
8. . . . has been built you can cross the High Street safely.
9. . . . such a dangerous airline that very few people used it.
10. . . . the superjet two hours to fly from London to New York.

Vocabulary Building

1. To get out of, to get on (with), to get over, to get on with, to get through, to get (someone) down, to get (something) back, to get into.

2. to get up, to get through, to get (someone) down, to get (something) back, to get on with, to get out of, to get over, to get on with, to get into.

UNIT THREE

Foundations

3. a Tom and Tony are Christopher's sons.
   b Christopher and Tom have jobs but Tony doesn't.
   c Yes.
   d Sympathetic.

4. c

5. (1) With (2) working/employed (3) as (4) for (5) if/when (6) who
   (7) down/along/up (8) at (9) but (10) long (11) work (12) just
   (13) It (14) had (15) out (16) but/though
   (17) house/place/lounge/sitting-room (18) day (19) for (20) man.

6. a qualify b sack c support d out of work e depressed f employed.

Exam Training

1. (b) phrasal verbs (c) word sets (d) compound words (e) opposites.

2. a unemployed b permanent c failure d decreased/dropped e part-time
   f cash g pension h salary i loan j debt.

3. The first exercise tested opposites, the second tested word sets.

Grammar Building

3. a such b so c so d such e so f too g so h such i so j too.

Revision Transformations

1. ... such a low salary that he demanded a pay rise.
2. ... so/as interesting as her other one.
3. ... too unhealthy/ill to become a soldier.
4. ... more work.
5. ... working abroad was so exciting that he never came back.
6. ... so big/large (that) she didn't need to work.

7. . . . was too short for her to visit her aunt in Australia.
    . . . was so short that she couldn't visit her aunt in Australia.
8. . . . the most marvellous opportunity I've ever had.
9. . . . as hard as Toshi.
10. . . . the training course to be more interesting.

UNIT FOUR

Foundations

3. a The topic of the first paragraph is the story of how life on Earth had ended.
      The topic of the second is how people would perhaps return to Earth on day.
    b The 'Colony' is somewhere in space. 'Home' is the planet Earth.

4. b

5. (1) several/some/two (2) him (3) been (4) But/However (5) the/those
    (6) last (7) up/flying/back (8) stopped (9) they (10) had (11) their
    (12) would (13) that (14) over/above/on/in (15) his (16) from/off
    (17) would/could (18) that/which (19) again/more (20) back/them

Exam Training

1. Possible answers:
    friendly, unfriendly, friendliness, unfriendliness, friendless, friendlessness,
    friendship, overfriendly.

2. Possible answers:
    a dis/unable   unhappy   disloyal   non-smoker   immature
       uncertain   un/dislike impossible   inconvenient   improper
       incapable   illogical   irresponsible independent   unkind
       dishonest   disagree   irrelevant   illegal

    You use *im-* in front of *p* and *m*
             il- in front of l
             ir- in front of *r*

    These beginnings give words a negative meaning.

    b ability   encouragement   probability   possibility
       development   responsibility employment   capability
       maturity   government   agreement

    These endings make nouns.

c dryness   hardship   friendship   friendliness   companionship
   childhood   childishness sadness   happiness   neighbourhood
   widowhood   ownership   freshness   staleness   shortness
   softness   lightness   kindness

These endings make nouns.

d actor   player   worker   governor owner
   employer   pianist   violinist guitarist typist
   writer   physicist biologist

These endings make nouns describing people's jobs.

e blacken   popularize simplify broaden   solidify
   sadden   clarify   harden   soften   lighten
   shorten   lengthen   legalize freshen

These endings make verbs.

f beautiful   dusty   forgetful   icy   friendly/less
   childish/less hopeful/less foolish   joyful/less   careful/less
   sunny   windy   rainy

These endings make adjectives.

3. a 1 beautiful 2 carefully 3 Childhood 4 length 5 musician(s)
       6 actress 7 resignation 8 energetic

    b 1 incapable 2 dislike 3 unhappily 4 irresponsibility
       5 carelessness 6 unwise 7 disagree 8 disabled

Extension

Possible answers:

intelligence   weakness   strength   (un)certainty
(un)fairness   (dis)honesty   (un)kindness   (dis)loyalty
truth   sadness   cruelty   (ir)responsibility
(in)equality   (un)happiness   stupidity   (un)friendliness/friendship
wisdom   (im)patience   cleverness   freedom

Grammar Building

1.

Sentence	Present simple	Present continuous	Going to	Will
a				will arrive
b	are		are going to crash	
c		is arriving		
d	reaches			
e	's			'll get
f			's going to meet	
g		'm visiting		
h	is			

You can't change any of these verb forms without changing the meaning, although the changes are generally quite small.

2. You'll probably use these verb forms:
   a Present simple – for future timetables
   b Going to – for intentions
      Present continuous – for plans
   c Will – for predictions about the future
   d Going to – for future actions or states that are almost certain to happen because of present circumstance
   e Will – for spontaneous decisions about the future
   f Present continuous – for plans

Revision Transformations

1. . . . Victor doesn't come soon he will/he'll miss the plane.
2. . . . travel on a spaceship you will probably feel sick.
3. . . . the soldiers get to the space station it will be too late to stop the rocket from leaving.
4. . . . there will be an economic crisis in about six months' time.
5. . . . going to Paris next Tuesday.
6. . . . leaves/goes/is at 3.25 p.m.
7. . . . we arrive at Houston we will have lunch.
8. . . . the weather is good the launch of the balloon will not take place.
9. . . . going to learn/learning Spanish next year.
10. . . . arrive at the airport, please collect your hand-luggage.

Vocabulary Building

1.
angry	at/about/with	happy	at/about/with
aware	of	worried	about
good	at/with	anxious	about
envious	about/of	scared	of
terrified	of/about/at	afraid	of
furious	at/with/about	impatient	with
frightened	at/about/of	jealous	of
bad	at/with		

2.   aware, good, bad.

3.   anger, envy, terror, fury, fright, happiness, worry, anxiety, a scare, fear, impatience, jealousy.

UNIT FIVE

Foundations

1.   Pot-holing, hang-gliding, knitting, skateboarding, puppet-making, computer games.

4.   b

6.   (1) happens/occurs (2) us/you (3) what (4) his/this (5) night (6) by (7) In (8) less (9) should (10) body/animal

8.   (11) that/which (12) before (13) in (14) be (15) were (16) catch (17) some (18) this/that (19) by/all (20) when/if

9.   Animals: hyenas, lions, vultures, buffalo.
      Animal noises: howling, screaming, roaring.

   Other possible animals and their noises: cats miaow, dogs bark, cows moo, horses neigh, mice squeak, pigs snort or grunt.

Exam Training

1.   – There are eight sentences to complete.
      – The bars mean that a word or words are missing.
      – When there is a bar, you have to add the missing word(s).

2. You can add as many words as you need to make a correct sentence. You will probably never need more than two or three.
   - Some possible answers:

Nouns:	—	Pronouns:	it, that
Adverbs:	—	Conjunctions:	so, and
Verbs:	will/can see	Prepositions:	from, on, in,
	would have been		for, with, of
Articles:	the, a		

   - Most of the verbs are written in the infinitive form, e.g. *see, be, stay*. You have to put them into the correct form.

3. - Mary is probably Aunt Jill's niece. Judging by the language of the letter their relationship is probably quite formal.
   - To thank her for taking her to the theatre.
   - Past events: seeing her aunt, catching the train, going to the theatre. No present events. Future events: her exams, her next letter, a future visit.

4. a It was lovely to see you last week.
   b I am/was sorry I had to rush to catch the/my last train and we couldn't talk any longer.
   c I would like to thank you for inviting me to the play at the Theatre Royal, which I really enjoyed.
   d I always love/have always loved Shakespeare and/so it was wonderful to see a production of one of his most famous plays.
   e I am sure it will help me in/with my English exams that/which I take/am taking next month.
   f I will write you a longer letter when all the/my exams are over.
   g We would also like to come and visit you when the weather gets better.
   h Thank you very much once again for everything.

5. - The writer of this letter doesn't know the person he/she is writing to. They have a formal relationship.
   - To complain about a Leisure Centre.
   - Expressions of time: yesterday, first, two hours, then, after, while, By then, again.

   a I am/I'm writing to complain about the service at the Dizzy Castle Leisure Centre, where I went with my three children yesterday.
   b First, we had to wait (for) two hours to get in as/because/since only one entrance was open.
   c Then, there were such long queues (that) it was impossible for us to go on anything.
   d After a while we all needed an ice-cream but the ice-cream shop was closed.
   e We bought (some) sandwiches instead but they were so disgusting (that) we threw them away/they were disgusting so we threw them away.
   f By then we were so angry and upset (that) we decided to go home/very angry and upset so we decided to go home.
   g We will certainly not/We are certainly not going to visit Dizzy Castle again.

Grammar Building

1. Column 1 = verbs + infinitive with *to*
   Column 2 = verbs + either form
   Column 3 = verbs + *-ing* form

2. (1) playing   (2) to be   (3) to do   (4) playing   (5) sitting   (6) doing
   (7) having   (8) to stop/stopping   (9) feeling   (10) doing   (11) to study
   (12) to go   (13) to do   (14) to stay

3. (1) shouting   (2) sitting   (3) to put   (4) picking   (5) putting
   (6) to collect   (7) to get   (8) to collect   (9) put/putting   (10) stop/stopping
   (11) worrying   (12) to remember   (13) looking   (14) putting

Extension

1. doing   2. doing   3. to be, being   4. to do, to do
5. to do, to do   6. being, to be   7. to do, to do   8. doing, to do
9. to buy   10. doing, doing

Revision Transformations

1. . . . our/us going windsurfing tomorrow/the next day.
2. . . . cleaning.
3. . . . cheating at cards.
4. . . . smoking in restaurants.
5. . . . us swimming in the sea.
6. . . . paying the bill.
7. . . . him to go home early.
8. . . . to go to the cinema.
9. . . . seeing that football match.
10. . . . (on) missing the ball.

Vocabulary Building

2. amusing, amusement, delightful, enjoyable, enjoying, enjoyment, entertaining, entertainment, likeable, liking.

UNIT SIX

Foundations

1. a head   b neck   c shoulder   d chest   e elbow   f wrist   g waist
   h thigh   i knee   j shin   k ankle   l foot.

2. a lungs b heart c liver d kidneys e stomach f appendix g intestines

4. a That it started when a man with a headache accidentally dropped a rock on
      his foot and found that his headache stopped.
    b Pien Chueh was a Chinese man who practised acupuncture and other
      alternative medical treatments.

5. c

6. (1) so (2) one (3) on (4) started/began (5) But/However (6) was
    (7) made (8) ago (9) for (10) when (11) ill (12) for (13) being
    (14) saw/realized/noticed/established/found (15) one (16) other (17) able
    (18) up (19) take/drink/have (20) did

7. The clues to blank number (11) are in the same sentence as the blank and also
    in the following ones. The words 'was very seriously' show us that the missing
    word must be an adjective; the following sentences tell us that the Prince was
    ill.

Extension

First, she must eat to make herself stronger and to increase her blood pressure.
Then, she must drink Herb B to decrease her temperature. Finally, she must have
acupuncture. Then she will be ready for the operation.

Exam Training

1. The sentences you have to write are very often questions.

2. Possible answers:
    (1) What's the matter?/What's the problem?
    (2) Just how long have you had it?/how long has this been going on?
    (3) Do you get/have/feel it all the time?
    (4) What sort/kind/type of (a) pain is it?/What does it feel like?
    (5) Have you (ever) had it before?
    (6) What do you (usually/normally) eat?

3. Some possible questions:
    a How much is it/are the potatoes/they?
      How much does it/do they cost?
    b How long have you lived here/spoken English?
    c Shall we go and see 'Gone With The Wind'?
    d Is it sunny?/Is the weather nice?
    e What's he/John like?
    f Can I try those shoes on, please?/Have you got any yellow socks?

g When are you going skiing?
h How many children have you got/are there?/Do you have any children?
i Are you watching/going to watch TV/television tonight?
j Excuse me, could you tell me the time, please/Do you know what the time is?/Have you got the time?

5. The informal dialogue is 'Two friends on the phone'. 'Two businessmen on the phone' is a more formal dialogue.
    Some differences in the language of the two dialogues:

Informal	More formal
Hi	good morning
Fine	Very well
that would be great	How very kind
at your place	at your house
See you	I'll look forward to seeing you this evening
Bye	Goodbye

One way of completing the informal dialogue:
B   – Hi, it's Tony.
      – Fine. And you?
      – Would you like to come round for a meal tonight?
      – About eight.
      – Good. See you.

One way of completing the more formal dialogue:
B   – Good morning, this is George Thompson.
      – Very well, thank you. And you?
      – I was wondering if/whether you'd like to come to dinner tonight at my house.
      – Eight o'clock at my house.
      – Yes. Goodbye.

6. Some possible answers:
    (1) Tell us about aromatherapy/what aromatherapy is.
    (2) And what is it particularly used for/recommended for?
    (3) How do you use/apply/take the oils?
    (4) Who first thought of aromatherapy?/started aromatherapy?/discovered aromatherapy?
    (5) And what did they use them for?
    (6) So does it really help people relax?/it help when you're feeling tense?

Grammar Building

1. Possible answers:
    Mr Thompson's problem – baldness. The doctor's advice – Brandex can be effective in treating baldness, but not to use if elderly.

Mrs Troops' problem – son may be colour blind. The doctor's advice – take
son to doctor to find out if colour blind. If he is, tell teachers.

2. Verbs in passive: is used, has been sold, was discovered, has been shown, is
applied, is not recommended, are (often) used.
Modal verbs with passive infinitive: can be caused, can be detected.

3. Report b
In b there are more verbs in the passive than in a. The effect of this is to make
report b seem much more formal and anonymous.

4. Generally speaking, the sentences in the passive are more anonymous, formal
and official.
Some possible answers:
a The first sentence suggests that the speaker does not necessarily agree with
'some people'.
The second sentence suggests that this is the general belief of the majority of
doctors.
b The first sentence suggests that 'we' have failed to diagnose the illness.
The second sentence suggests that nobody could possibly diagnose the
illness.
c The first sentence suggests that the speaker is accusing someone.
The second sentence suggests that the speaker does not know who robbed
her/him.
d The first sentence suggests that the speaker is possibly making a subtle
suggestion to the listener.
In the second sentence, the speaker is giving a direct command.
e In the first sentence, the speaker is admitting her/his own inability to do
something.
In the second sentence, the speaker suggests that nobody could possibly do
anything.
f The first sentence is probably a notice in a big public place.
The second sentence is a polite spoken request.
The third sentence is like the first, but more severe.
The fourth sentence is a polite notice in a public place.

6. a are treated/can be/may be treated   b were discovered
c must/should not be taken   d can/may be prevented   e will be found
f should not be/ought not to be/must not be drunk   g is/can be/may be used
h is said

Revision Transformations

1. ... to build a large new hospital were drawn up three years ago.
2. ... been painted yet.
3. ... were tested last week.

4.   . . . must be reduced.
5.   . . . has still not been found.
6.   . . . was shown the way to the hospital by a woman in a green hat.
7.   . . . is said to be bad for you.
8.   . . . was advised (by her doctor) to give up smoking immediately.
9.   . . . need to be/must be exercised regularly if we want to stay fit.
10.   . . . my teeth checked every six months.

Vocabulary Building

2.   to come off a diet, to cut down on smoking, etc., to get over/to go down with measles, etc., to go on a diet/smoking, to look after yourself/your health, to put on weight, to give up a diet/smoking, etc.

3.   Some possible answers:
cleanly, unclean, uncleanliness, digestive, digestion, indigestion, digestible, indigestible, efficiency, inefficient, inefficiency, painful, painfully, painless, painlessness, painfulness, safely, unsafe, safety.

UNIT SEVEN

Foundations

2.   Things you do at school: cheating, homework, essay, history, maths, chemistry, biology, art, literature, gym, sports.
Types of assessment: homework, continuous assessment, report, tests, exam.
Places at school: classroom, library, gym, playground, science lab.
Descriptions of people: careless, hard-working, bored, intelligent, interesting, boring, lazy.

5.   a It probably comes from a radio talk rather than a newspaper or a magazine because its style is very direct and personal.
b What students eat and their performance at school.

6.   d

9.   (1) was   (2) these   (3) at   (4) all   (5) ate   (6) we
(7) have/contain/include   (8) groups   (9) one   (10) which/that
(11) but/yet   (12) took/had   (13) them   (14) a/any   (15) between
(16) had   (17) than   (18) it   (19) we   (20) are

Exam Training

1. a, b, c, d, g, h, i, j.

2. a The first kind of text describes four classes of students. The second kind
describes six different trips or excursions.
   b Their age, where their school is
   c See page 82.

4.

	TOWERS	BURTINGTON	ST THOMAS'	NELSON
SIZE OF CLASS	25	15	23	12
AGE OF STUDENTS	11	16	7	18
MALE/FEMALE	both	boys	both	girls
TOWN	central London	outer London	Reading	Oxford

6. a The first kind of text is about four proposals for new additions to the
buildings of St Barnabas' school and a proposal for a free trip. The second
kind of text describes the four school governors.
   b Mrs Green wants to sell food to the school's students and is keen on an
aspect of science.
Colonel Brown believes especially in exercise and working for things.
Patricia White writes books and has a child who will soon go to the school.
Kenneth Norton believes in exercise and a good scientific education and
doesn't support the library plan.

7.

	APPROVES OF	DISAPPROVES OF
MRS GREEN	selling her own food to the students astronomy	probably disapproves of canteen
COLONEL BROWN	lots of exercise	anyone getting anything free
PATRICIA WHITE	might approve of library as she writes books herself	
KENNETH NORTON	healthy students a good scientific education	the library scheme

Grammar Building

1. If the books weren't so old, I would/could read them.
   If the lessons weren't so long, I wouldn't go to sleep.
   If the the desks were comfortable, I would be able to/could/would sit still.
   If the school wasn't/weren't far from home, I wouldn't have to take a bus.
   If the teacher liked me, I wouldn't get bad marks.

2. If I passed my exam, I could/would get a job in a bank.
   If I got a job in a bank, I would earn a lot of money.
   If I earned a lot of money, I could/would buy a yacht.
   If I bought a yacht, I could/would travel round the world.
   If I travelled round the world, I would have to take a long holiday.
   If I took a long holiday, I would lose my job.
   If I lost my job, I would be short of money.
   If I was/were short of money, I could/would sell the yacht.
   If I sold the yacht, I would/could buy a farm.
   If I bought a farm, I would/could grow the best grapes in the country.
   If I grew the best grapes in the country, I would make a lot of money.
   If I made a lot of money, I could/would buy an aeroplane.

3. d, c, g, e, h, b, j, f, i, a.
   d If the hall hadn't been empty, the headmaster wouldn't have seen me.
   c If anyone else had been there, he wouldn't have invited me into his study.
   g If it hadn't been urgent, he wouldn't have had to ask someone quickly.
   e If his daughter hadn't been busy, she could have gone to India.
   h If she had been able to use her ticket, he wouldn't have given it to me.
   b If my parents hadn't been at work, I would have phoned them.
   j If I had asked my parents then, they would have said no.
   f If I hadn't already had the ticket, my parents would have stopped me going.
   i If they had tried to stop me, I would have disobeyed them.
   a If the bus hadn't been late, I wouldn't have gone to India.

4. (1) will pay   (2) didn't study   (3) wouldn't pay   (4) wouldn't be able
   (5) wouldn't have studied   (6) would/should choose   (7) wanted
   (8) will give   (9) will/shall never speak   (10) became   (11) would be able
   (12) had known   (13) wouldn't have gone out   (14) had wanted

Revision Transformations

1. . . . he had been well/hadn't been ill, he would have taken his exam.
2. . . . had been a gym, we would have played sports at school.
3. . . . would speak French much better if we had a language laboratory.
4. . . . get some computers if it could afford them.
5. . . . his chemistry marks had been good/better, they would have let him study medicine.

6. ... had the right qualifications, we could get jobs.
7. ... had been a chemistry teacher, we would have studied chemistry.
8. ... the exam had been essential, he wouldn't have taken it.
9. ... didn't strongly believe in science, our school wouldn't have an excellent science lab.
10. ... spend some time in France, I won't improve my French accent.

Vocabulary Building

4. Some possible answers:
   careful, careless, overconfident, forgetful, unforgettable, unprepared, overprepared, successful, unsuccessful, teachable, unteachable.

UNIT EIGHT

Foundations

1. A Scotland   B England   C Wales
2. 1 Stratford   2 Cambridge   3 Edinburgh   4 London
4. The weather, opening hours and eating.
5. a
6. (1) of   (2) few   (3) be   (4) the   (5) never   (6) should/must
   (7) take/bring   (8) other   (9) close   (10) break/rest   (11) As
   (12) but/though/although   (13) find/see   (14) does   (15) a   (16) they/these
   (17) good   (18) can/may   (19) let   (20) have
7. a changeable, rainy, sunny, hot, cold.
   b tasty, good value for money, good, varied, cheap.

Exam Training

1. b and c

2. a 2

   = wind speed and direction   = sunny periods

   = temperature   = sunny periods with light rain

   3 The sunniest, warmest and driest areas will be Wales and south-west England.
   b 1 England and Wales   2 Scotland

   c 1 Railway station
      2 Place of interest open to the public/Important building
      3 Between 2 and 2½ miles, or nearly 4 kilometres
      4 Piccadilly, St James's St, Pall Mall, Constitution Hill
      5 The Serpentine Gallery or Speakers Corner
      6 Any of the following:
         Museum of Mankind, Royal Academy, St James's Palace, Marlborough House, Cabinet War Rooms, No. 10 Downing St, Westminster Abbey, Royal Horticultural Halls, Westminster Cathedral, Westminster Theatre, Victoria and Albert Museum, Brompton Oratory, Harrods.

3.   Molly and George Turner – *42nd Street*
     Françoise Martin and Beatrice Gautier – one of the Shakespeare plays
     Jill and Frank Marsden – *How the Other Half Loves* or *The Mousetrap*
     The students from Scotland – Marcel Marceau or *The Sleeping Beauty*

Grammar Building

1.   a insist, tell
     b advise, recommend, suggest, warn
     c inform, tell

2.   a I will/advise/recommend/suggest to my friend to bring both light and warm clothes for the summer.
     b I will warn/tell my friend not to forget to drive on the left.
     c I will advise/recommend/suggest to my friend to stay in a bed and breakfast.
     d I will advise/warn/recommend my friend not to eat in restaurants unless she/he has a lot of money.
     e I will tell/inform my friend (that) shops close on Wednesday afternoons.
     f I will tell my friend to visit Cambridge/I will insist my friend visits Cambridge because it's beautiful.
     g I will advise/recommend my friend to stay outside London.
        I will suggest to my friend that he/she stays outside London.
     h I will tell/warn my friend not to drink and drive.
     i I will inform/tell my friend (that) you have to leave pets in quarantine.
     j I will tell my friend to remember that Indian restaurants are generally cheap and good.
     k I will suggest to my friend to eat in pubs as they're very good and cheap.
        I will suggest (that) my friend eats in pubs as they're very good and cheap.
     l I will tell/warn my friend that pub opening hours vary from pub to pub.

Revision Transformations

1.   . . . that Paul should go by ferry/Paul's going by ferry/to Paul to go by ferry/that Paul went by ferry.
2.   . . . not to go out late by myself.
3.   . . . me (that I needed) to take my umbrella.
4.   . . . not to park their cars on double yellow lines.

5. ... me he hadn't got any money left.
6. ... the class that Edinburgh was/is the capital of Scotland.
7. ... to let the passenger take guns into Britain.
8. ... that the bank closed/closes at three p.m.
9. ... her students to go to a pub when they went to England.
10. ... said to/told her friend that it can/could rain a lot in Britain in the summer.

Vocabulary Building

1. b at once   c at any moment   d at times   e at last   f at short notice

2. a At times   b at any rate   c at short notice   4 at once   5 At last

4. strong, confident, courageous, healthy, patient, proud, wise
    Opposites: weak, insecure/lacking in confidence, cowardly, sick/ill, impatient, humble/ashamed, foolish.

UNIT NINE

Foundations

3. The press

4. a An organization in which children work to produce their own newspaper.
    b It shows some of the children conducting interviews.

6. (1) published/printed   (2) the   (3) well   (4) to   (5) point
    (6) what/which   (7) on   (8) interested   (9) as   (10) are   (11) most
    (12) by   (13) such   (14) in   (15) write/print/publish/produce   (16) number
    (17) going   (18) next   (19) be   (20) programme/station

Exam Training

1. Gordon Smith is against: noisy, spoils peace, upsets older tourists.
    Mick Tagger is for: gives young people an opportunity to express themselves and feel 'wanted'.
    Joan Bennet is for: knows her own children would enjoy it (but thinks it shouldn't just be for young people).
    Leader of the Council is against: has received many complaints, is worried because of elections and opposition of Gordon Smith.

2. a B   b D   c C   d E   e A

3. a Firstly   B because   C What's more

Grammar Building

2. a The old man asked where he had put his keys.
    b A stranger asked if there was/is a garage near there/here.
    c The film director asked when they were filming the snow scene.
    d The reporter asked if this/the plan would really create new jobs.
    e Mary asked if I/you/etc. would like to come to dinner tonight/that night.
    f The actress asked if we/they had met before.
    g The young man asked me if he could help me with my suitcase.
    h John's mother asked why we/they didn't go to the cinema instead.
    i The taxi driver asked if I/you/etc. was/were sure the theatre was/is in Green Street.
    j The teacher asked why ice floats/floated.

3. a . . . where he had put his keys.
    b . . . if/whether there was/is a garage near there/here.
    c . . . when they were filming the snow scene.
    d . . . whether the/this plan would really create new jobs.
    e . . . me/us, etc. to dinner tonight/that night.
    f . . . if/whether we/they had met before.
    g . . . to carry my suitcase.
    h . . . that we should go to the cinema instead/our/us going to the cinema instead.
    i . . . whether/if the theatre is/was in Green Street.
    j . . . why ice floats/floated.

Vocabulary Building

1. BOOK: shop, case, stall, seller, festival.
    FILM: director, show, set, seller, festival, producer, star.
    RADIO: programme, show, advertisement, station, set, announcer, broadcast, producer, aerial, star.
    TELEVISION: director, programme, show, advertisement, station, set, satellite, seller, announcer, broadcast, producer, aerial, star.

3. announcer, announcing, announcement, advertise, advertising, advertiser, advertisement, editing, editor, journalism, journalist, publisher, publishing, publicize, reporter, reporting.

PRACTICE PAPER ONE

1. (1) growing/increasing (2) it (3) than (4) not (5) but (6) the (7) them
   (8) only (9) to (10) go/travel/move (11) build (12) where (13) small/low
   (14) with (15) made (16) there (17) was (18) In (19) out (20) within

2. a . . . still at university.
   b . . . cry for help wasn't heard (by anybody)/was heard by nobody.
   c . . . going on holiday in the summer to working for extra money.
   d . . . I could live/lived in a house like that.
   e . . . the weather was bad we enjoyed ourselves in the mountains.
   f . . . hadn't encouraged me I wouldn't have applied for the job.
   g . . . from going to school yesterday by f.u/by f.u from going to school
   yesterday.
   h . . . if it was still raining.
   i . . . (that) the house was so big.
   j . . . to pay the bill.

3. a childhood b lengthen c handful d overcooked e resignation

4. a decreased b weakness c boring d generous e saving

5. a I am writing to enquire about the courses (that) you run in your school in
   the summer.
   b First of all, I'd/I would be grateful if you would/could tell me the cost of the
   courses.
   c Then, I'd/I would also like to know what kind of accommodation you
   provide.
   d Is you school residential or do you find us rooms with English families?
   e If you have a brochure I wonder if you could send me one?
   f I have already studied/already been studying English for five years.
   g I would be/I am particularly interested in intensive courses of/for/in business
   English.
   h I look forward to hearing from you and thank you in advance for your
   co-operation.

6. In my opinion Jenny Matthews will probably take her Japanese friend to Green's
   Vegetarian Restaurant because it is cheap. The good music and the lively
   atmosphere will make it an exciting and different night out for her friend.
   I think that Michael Barnet will choose to go to Chez Catherine. He will
   want to impress his new girlfriend with the good food and the romantic
   atmosphere. As he is a company director, he will probably be able to afford
   the high prices.
   As for Ana and Pedro Gomez, they will probably go to Da Gino because it
   is open late and has the kind of noisy but friendly atmosphere that they enjoy.
   Although it is not a vegetarian restaurant, it will probably provide some
   vegetarian food for Ana.
   Finally, Jill Edwards and her friends will probably choose Kyoto Japanese

Restaurant because it is open late enough for them. It is also quiet, so they can discuss their holiday plans. The excellent Japanese food is also likely to please and interest them.

PRACTICE PAPER TWO

1. (1) with   (2) until/till/to   (3) main/principal/chief   (4) went   (5) after
    (6) before/previously   (7) to   (8) but/though   (9) jobs   (10) own
    (11) get/have/receive   (12) same   (13) from/against   (14) they/women
    (15) not   (16) their   (17) choose   (18) for   (19) such   (20) staying.

2. a . . . seen his parents for ten years.
    b . . . I went to the dentist.
    c . . . went to bed at 3 a.m.
    d . . . warm/hot enough to go outside without a coat.
    e . . . Tom to look for a new job.
    f . . . having spent/spending so much money.
    g . . . does Janet speak Chinese, (but) she also speaks Arabic.
    h . . . loveliest beach I've ever seen,' said Jane.
    i . . . mustn't/can't smoke in cinemas.
    j . . . can be eaten directly from the packet.

3. a in   b back   c up   d round   e up

4. a roof   b garage   c rent   d garden/balcony   e heating

5. (1) How was your holiday?
    (2) what went wrong/what was wrong with it?
    (3) Had you been there before?
    (4) . . . are you going/are you thinking of going/are you planning to go?
    (5) Where did you go/Where was that?
    (6) . . . you read about it in a brochure/you find it through a travel agent/you find it yourselves?

6. I think Arlette Menle will choose the 'Learning Centre' because she needs to study English for her work and the 'Learning Centre' has business English classes. It also has small classes which she would probably like. As she is a managing director she would also probably have enough money to be able to pay the high fees the school charges.

    Yannis Spiridis will probably choose Buckley Manor because it is the only school he can afford. All the others would probably be too expensive for him. He would also be the same age as the other students at the school who are between the ages of seven and eighteen.

    The best choice for Marguerite Lanson is Locksley Hall because it has classes for all ages. It also has special classes for literature which will interest her. Because the school is near the sea will be able to get fresh fish to eat, and she will enjoy that.